Community
and
Spiritual
Transformation

Community
and
Spiritual
Transformation

Religion and Politics in a Communal Age

Gibson Winter

CROSSROAD • NEW YORK

1989

The Crossroad Publishing Company
370 Lexington Avenue, New York, N.Y. 10017

Printed in the United States of America

Library of Congress Cataloging-in-Publication Data

Winter, Gibson.
    Community and spiritual transformation : religion and
politics in a communal age / Gibson Winter.
        p.   cm.
    ISBN 0-8245-0960-9
    1. Religious ethics.   2. Social ethics.   I. Title.
BJ1188.W56   1989
291.5—dc20   89-33645
                                                          CIP

Contents

Foreword

In *Community and Spiritual Transformation,* Gibson Winter continues reflection on the motifs fundamental to his distinctive socio-moral and religious vision—love, justice, power, and community. Current Christian ethical discourse abounds in discussion of community, frequently bewailing its demise at the hands of secular modernity. The result is a social analysis which portrays confessional religious faith and the politics of public life as antagonists, with genuine morality the victim of the latter. By contrast, Winter insists on the indestructible character of the search for community. For him, the power of community is an ontic foundation of the ongoing search for life, and the fulcrum of moral struggle.

The ideological excesses of individualism, which others also decry, are for Winter less the fruit of erroneous doctrine than the results of past social decisions, decisions which may be rectified by religious and political transformation. While some excoriate the spirit of the age, Winter digs to discern both the constructive and destructive social and economic patterns of power operating in our midst. Religion and politics, profound expressions of human communitarian spirit and imagination, function at times to distort our communitarian existence. Even so, there are always emergent expressions of community in our midst that open the way toward authentic spiritual transformations in religion and politics. We cannot, he argues, turn away from the quest for either.

Winter's analysis provides important insights for differentiating between genuine and specious religious renewal and important criteria for the moral assessing of political change in the areas of personal, economic, and political life. Because he takes his cues from an aesthetic and process-oriented view of reality and attends to the learnings of community engaged in the struggle for justice—especially to women's voices and women's experience of community—he avoids the pitfall of perceiving change as the enemy of religious tradition. It is this uncompromising sensibility which makes the book particularly noteworthy.

One need not agree with all of the methodological moves that shape Gibson Winter's approach to Christian social ethics to be grateful for his thought-provoking and subtle assessment of our religious and political situation. At a time when concern for "communitarian ethics" often signals only a self-congratulatory reiteration of traditionalism in Christian ethical thought and practice, his persuasive argument for both complex discernment and unstinting engagement in public and moral reconstruction is very good news indeed!

BEVERLY W. HARRISON
The Carolyn Williams Beaird Professor
of Christian Ethics
Union Theological Seminary

Preface

As we approach the year 2000, there is evidence that we are on the threshold of a new era. We seem to have come to an important turning point in Western history. The signs of change are appearing on all sides. Competition in nuclear weaponry and in the global war system is proving wasteful and dangerous. Threats to the ozone layer, pollution of air and water, toxic poisoning of households, and damage to the rain forests are gradually awakening peoples to the threat of ecological disaster. Meanwhile, economic dislocations have thrown third world nations into hunger and malnutrition, burdening them with debts they cannot carry. As the interdependence of the global market has developed, the shared fate of all the peoples on earth has become a taken-for-granted fact. This is the climate in which a new approach to human civilization is beginning to take hold.

A sign of this new era is the religious revival that has spread throughout the world. Whether this revival is a symptom of the emerging world or a central force in its appearance has not been determined, since the two phenomena have appeared at once. However, religious revival in the last decades of the high-tech century was the last thing that one would have anticipated. Moreover, the revival is emerging in popular movements, giving rise to new spiritual forces outside the principal religious bodies. Many of the popular religious movements in Africa and South America are focused on personal salvation, but others are directly engaged with political issues. What appears, for example, to Western eyes as fundamentalist movements in Islam are actually renewals of Muslim faith and postcolonial life over against Western domination. By the same token, mainline religious bodies in the West have begun to engage in direct challenges to the political course of their own nation states. Whether in traditional or popular forms, the religious revival is changing the political as well as the spiritual landscape of our world.

Various tags have been attached to these new spiritual forces. There is talk of a "new age" or "an Aquarian age." Others speak of a postmodern world, referring to the passing of the nineteenth-century confidence in the capacity of science and technology to bring peace and justice to the world. However, the deeper spiritual content of this new era will remain obscure unless one penetrates to the profound nostalgia for community that pervades the world today. There is nostalgia for a communal life that is passing or has already passed under the conditions of a high-tech world. There is also a search for new communal forms that can reshape this high-tech world of impersonal markets and systems of compulsion. This communalism manifests itself in popular movements for liberation, democratic rule, human rights, and global justice. Thus, communal rebuilding is at least one, if not the most central, component of the new religious and political forces that are shaking the foundations of our world.

Community is the oldest of social forms, so far as one can tell from the record. Whether in hunting and gathering groups or households and villages, peoples have survived and reproduced in communal networks. In this sense, communal revival is simply carrying on the age-old work of human survival. Humans are communal beings from birth to death. They suffer and even perish when their communal bonds are frayed or destroyed. However, this central reality of community was displaced in recent centuries, at least in the West and in the parts of the world that the West has dominated. Communal networks continued to sustain personal life, but bonds between parents and children, neighbor and neighbor, friends, and workers were weakened. The achievements of the individual were elevated to first place in neighborhood, school, and workplace. The interdependence of work and culture, of national life and global relations, was played down and even concealed. The age of the individual brought a dynamic drive for success and a gradual weakening of the fabric of human communities. This led to the relegation of the weak, vulnerable, disabled, old, and ill to gray areas of deteriorated cities or to the streets and grates of the urban areas. Despite these corrosive forces, personal networks continued to nurture children, pass on linguistic and cultural heritage, and to some extent ameliorate the impact of an impersonal market-driven world. This is the context in which a nostalgia for community and a profound search for spiritual and communal renewal has taken root in our time.

Communal renewal in the new era has a special character. It cannot be a return to older communal forms, though many values from those forms need to be carried forward into the new societies. Family patterns, health care, organization of work, modes of political participation, and cultural opportunities will be restructured in more equitable and humane forms. Global connections will take on a more balanced and just pattern of exchange in which all can share. The meaning of personal life will be liberated from the distorted preoccupation with personal advantage. Bonds with the natural world will be rebuilt in ways that can enhance human life while preserving its fragile environment.

A communal interpretation of our changing times is far from self-evident. There are many different interpretations among social critics. Some see our world moving into ever deepening conflict and mutual destruction. Others believe the continued spread of impersonal technical arrangements will approach something like Orwell's *1984* by the year 2000. The usual interpretation is that things will continue much as they are, with gradual progress in standard of life and greater capacity to cope with environmental and economic problems.

A communal interpretation of the present situation is both pessimistic and optimistic. It envisions the human as an artistic, creative species, capable of adaptation to incredibly difficult circumstances. It also recognizes the human tendency to repeat again and again patterns of behavior that are proving destructive. These obsessions seem to be rooted in a "faith" structure that is hard to shake, even when evil is at the doorstep. John Wilson once noted that the Egyptian decline seemed to be rooted in their preoccupation with death. In this respect, the West may fail to meet its challenge through excessive concern for accumulation. Rather than settling for a mechanical repetition of fruitless accumulation or plunging into adventurous change, the communal vision unfolds the truly personal and creative elements in the human species.

It is this communal vision that is explored in the present volume. To this extent, this volume carries the initial inquiry in *Liberating Creation* into the artistic quality of human existence. Here, however, artistic vision is carried farther, into the poetic, metaphoric quality of the society people create in their loving, working, and deciding.

This communal interpretation of the present struggle begins with some indicators of the emerging communal reality. The first chapter traces the communal quality of the religious movements that now interact with political bodies. It becomes clear in this examination that communalism has a variety of forms in these religious movements. In the second chapter, the communal reality of personal and interpersonal life is unfolded, taking the contemporary controversy over abortion as illuminating the heart of the matter. No attempt is made to resolve the difficulties surrounding this public issue, but the interpersonal and moral dimensions are unpacked from the decisions of women confronting this question. The moral aspects of interpersonal life are then considered in more detail in the third chapter, where the moral web is viewed as the deeper side of the inward bonding of all of personal life. The argument then turns to the institutional side of community, for communal being is both personal and organizational: whereas life forces flow in interpersonal networks, the skeleton that supports or inhibits that flow of life is the institutional structure. Both personal and institutional patterns express the communal reality of human life; consequently, the fourth chapter turns to the organization of work as central to the institutions that support or damage personal life. This brings the story of communal rebuilding into the political arena. The struggle for a stable economy and a secure world is played out in the political field, or it is hampered by the failure of political bodies. Hence, the fifth chapter considers the movement from the minimal state of the market era to a democratic communalism in which the concerns of human life can become central to the political process. The final chapter returns more explicitly to the religious movements of our time, exploring transformations in belief and practice that are now emerging. In some ways, these transformations in religious life are the most radical changes that have occurred since the Reformation. Some of the broad lines of those innovations are examined in the final chapter.

The new communal age could not be so clearly outlined if it had not already come upon the scene. Much that is argued here is drawn from everyday knowledge and experience. The remarkable fact is that the market mentality has been able to suppress the communal reality of persons despite the scientific and practical evidence to the contrary. Thus, the argument is rather an uncovering of basic realities that have been too long concealed; indeed, it is a recovery in many ways of claims that social philosophers and theologians have been making for a century. In this sense, the text tries to retell the story of human survival that is recorded in our sacred texts and our classics, a story that needs to be played out on the new stage that a high-tech world has created.

Chapter One

Movements of Communal Transformation

Social and political instability often sparks movements of spiritual renewal. Monastic movements spread throughout the Roman Empire in the period of its decline. Innumerable lay movements of spiritual transformation appeared in Europe during the breakup of the feudal synthesis. Rapid changes and instability have generated similar movements throughout the globe in our own time. Conservative movements in Islam reflect resistance to transformations in traditional ways of life. In a somewhat different way, religious movements in Asia are challenging dictatorial regimes and attempting to establish a semblance of democratic justice. Religious communities in South and Central America have participated in struggles against elites who have controlled economic and political life for centuries.

These vital movements of spiritual renewal have come rather unexpectedly upon the political scene. The twentieth century prided itself upon its *Realpolitik*. Social critics had been writing for a generation about the "end of ideology," by which they meant the resolution of economic and political issues through a kind of means-end rationality. This was to be the century of technical management of human problems. Meanwhile, deep currents of unrest had been undermining this managerial world. Poor people were getting poorer, while riches were extracted from their lands. Older customs of local and national life were being destroyed, and nothing of value was being substituted except the promise of "development" in the future. Even the kind of development that was emerging offered little in the way of personal or communal stability, except to privileged elites. Within a generation, the world was plunged into a moral and spiritual crisis that was not to be suppressed by managerial skills.

There is at least one basic reason why religious concerns surface in periods of radical instability. Religion symbolizes a people's sense of identity, of who they are as a people. A sense of identity emerges in the communities that surround and support a people. Identity is forged out of experiences that reveal to us who we are, how we can negotiate our way in the world, and what we can hope for in that journey. In this sense, identity is a temporal event that is constantly being formed. As we mature, we achieve a certain stability in our self-understanding, a certain character and way of coping with our lives. It is similar with peoples, except that communities and nations achieve their identity over long periods of time through crucial experiences and symbolic interpretations. Whether personal or communal, a sense of identity is a temporal or historical phenomenon, giving continuity amid change. For this reason, a sense of identity is best encapsulated in stories, both personal and communal. Stories are the way in which we gain a sense of the whole of our temporal experience, interpreting what has happened to us in the past and outlining the kind of future we anticipate. Stories deal with the whole of our experience. That totality can never be subsumed under an idea or scheme, because the past recedes into unfathomable mystery even as the future opens out upon possibilities that cannot be taken in hand. Our identities, our stories as persons and peoples, are the expressions of our religious way of being and understanding. (Here *religion* is understood in the very broad sense of how we come to terms with our origins and our destiny, where we have come from and why, where we are going and in what way.) Moreover, our stories try to come to terms with the difficulties and tragedies that have punctuated our lives, fitting them so far as possible in some meaningful way into the sense of continuity that we strive to achieve. Our sense of national identity in the United States is built around just such stories and symbols. We celebrate the times of founding, the struggle for independence, and the establishment of the Constitution. We do our best to live with the tragic mistreatment of American Indians and importation of slaves from Africa. In this sense, our stories have to include petitions for forgiveness as well as gratitude for gifts and accomplishments.

For those who confine "religion" to communities that profess particular creeds or affirm a deity, this may seem a strange way to interpret religion. However, religion in the most general sense may or may not involve ideas of God or gods. Religion is the way in which persons and communities understand and live their stories in a confusing and changing world. Religion is first and foremost the way in which we symbolize our journey on this earth; to this extent, religion binds persons into communities and joins communities or tribes into larger, spiritual realities. Our personal stories are actually communal stories, for they express the ways in which we have grown in our families and communities. Religion in this broad sense is already there when we are born. It is an encompassing story of our people's origins and destiny, a narrative that we begin to share in family and communal celebrations. A Memorial Day parade, perhaps one in which we have the chance to march, is already telling us about those whose deaths have made our lives possible, binding us to a community that we have yet to understand. Religion, thus, is the way in which temporal beings symbolize and celebrate the whole of the human story that always exceeds their grasp.

Within this interpretation of religion, it is understandable that periods of radical instability would kindle religious fires. Established religious institutions may or may not be able to respond to such crises. The Constantinian church could not cope with the decline of the very empire to which it had submitted. The late Medieval church was too corrupt to cope with the breakup of its own synthesis. On the other hand, churches in the Philippines, Korea, South Africa, and Muslim communities in the Middle East have mobilized spiritual resources in their people's struggles. Sometimes religious institutions are so closely wedded to the established authorities that they cannot even sense the deep restlessness in a people's life. At other times, they are enough in touch with the suffering of the poor, as has happened in Latin America, that they can share that suffering and struggle. In any case, the shock waves from deep currents of instability can generate vital movements of spiritual life, even in eras that seem on the surface to be utterly without religious sensibility.

The crisis of personal and communal life in the United States and actually throughout the world is a consequence of the shattering impact of technical change and the erosion of communal solidarity. This is a public crisis of major proportions that has been building up over many generations. This public, communal character of the crisis has given a special quality to the religious responses. Whether directly or indirectly, the spiritual movements are wrestling with public, communal concerns. We shall give primary attention to the movements in the United States, though the public concern is evident in every part of the globe. In the Republic, the concern is with basic values of democracy and justice in local communities and national life. Even major religious institutions are focusing more and more on public questions. This is the distinctive mark of the movements for spiritual renewal. Perhaps it is no accident that two religious pastors ran as candidates for the presidency of the United States in 1988.

This public communal concern is very different from the monastic movements or lay revivals of earlier times. It is closest in character to the radical Reformation of communities like the Anabaptists. However, the present movements are not separatist but are attempting to impinge directly on the public life. In this sense, the center of gravity of spirituality in our time is the public sphere. This centering of broadly religious concern in the public realm is actually not a new phenomenon. It had already begun in the seventeenth century, when the nation states were taking their modern shape. Dutch, British, French, Spanish, and later German and Russian nationalisms were being forged. Whether it was Britannia or La France or Mother Russia or Der Vaterland, in each case a national religion was emerging. In the United States, this national movement was crystallized in the Declaration of Independence and the forging of the Constitution. From this time, the center of gravity of the broadly religious impulse would be around the origins and destiny of this new nation.

Prior to the seventeenth century, Christian institutions claimed a monopoly of the spiritual life. They persecuted any community or individual who challenged that hegemony. Muslims and Jews were treated as enemies or pariahs. With the new nationalisms, this monopoly was broken. Confessional bodies became one expression of religious life, and for many people not the most important. Actually, institutional religion joined forces with the new nationalisms in Europe, forming state churches. The sacred traditions of the European churches became the source of legitimation for the ambitions of the new nations. In the new American Republic, a balance was struck between the religion of the Republic and the religion of the denominations, as Sidney Mead described it many years ago.[1] Confessional bodies were given privileges and assumed responsibility for building moral character among the citizens. The public faith sustained national commitments to democracy and human rights. The age of public religion had made a place for confessional communities but broken their religious monopoly.

The secular hypothesis offered an alternative understanding of the emergence of national religions. In this view, societies became "secular" or nonreligious in the modern era. Secular states were godless, materialistic entities that had deserted the religious fold. Evangelical communities in the United States still use this language and refer to the activities of public schools as the imposition of "secular humanism" or godlessness on their children. This hypothesis presumes that confessional bodies have a monopoly on sacred realities. Whatever happens outside these faith communities is nonreligious. In fact, the hypothesis is not very persuasive, for European churches were emptied in the course of modernity, yet churches in the United States flourished. It may well be that the state churches of Europe created a climate in which national religious and confessional faiths were fused. The separation of church and state in the United States meant that confessional identification would have to involve affiliation with one or another faith community. In Europe and the United States, however, national religions had become the principal vehicles of sacred identity. This new phenomenon did not eliminate the importance of confessional bodies, as we shall see subsequently, but it did change the character of their tasks.

The erosion of communal bonds in the West has created serious conflicts within national religions. These tensions are surfacing in challenges by confessional bodies to accepted values in public life. However, some of the most dynamic challenges are coming from movements within the national life itself. Whether inside or outside confessional communities, these movements are either trying to recover older values in the life of the Republic or promote new directions for the national life. The movements can be grouped under three broad headings, although there is some overlap among them. The first is "fundamentalist communalism," a major force that has sparked an evangelical revival in all types of confessional bodies. In response to the instability of the era, this movement reflects an attempt to reach back to older moral values in the national life. "Private communalism," another expression, is widespread in confessional bodies and generally throughout the society. Like fundamentalism, it is radically individualistic but expresses itself in community activism, therapy or support groups, and more broadly in life-style communities. A third force at work in moral and spiritual renewal can be designated "public communalism." It is a broad challenge to the whole course of Western life, striving to bring older and newer values into some kind of harmony within economic and political life.

Two religious disclosures can be detected in these movements. First, in response to the erosion of community under the impact of Western high-tech culture and organization, the sacred reality of the communal being of the human is revealed. This communal being of persons has been radically suppressed in the modern world. Second, these movements raise basic questions about the religious values that shape nationalisms today. We shall also have to examine these challenges and the kind of future they project. However, it will first be important to clarify the character and range of these movements and the kinds of values which they are fostering.

Fundamentalist Communalism

Biblical literalism and fundamentalism are very old traditions in the confessional heritage of North America. However,

there are several new notes in the resurgence of fundamentalist movements. For one thing, as noted before, it is making its
impact on the public life of the United States, not only as nationalism but also in movements such as "right to life" and the
moral majority. Further, the evangelical preachers who have
promoted fundamentalism now have a crucial position in religious television. Evangelical and denominational bodies have
always played an indirect role in American politics. Now, however, they have intervened directly in the political arena
through agencies such as the National Conservative Political
Action Committee (NCPAC) and the Moral Majority. Moreover,
their interventions are largely on behalf of very traditional
communal values of family life and personal morality.

These shifts in the role of fundamentalism reflect the more
basic shift in the religious center of gravity from confessional
bodies to public life. The interdependence of life today means
that most communities experience the larger movements of
the society in work, media, and life-styles. Sectarian and denominational communities cannot escape this impact and now
have to work out their life of faith in the public arena. To this
extent, fundamentalism is following the course of American
life in a realistic fashion.

The struggle to establish prayer in public schools once again
has been high on the fundamentalist agenda. NCPAC solicited
support for the Reagan administration with this agenda. Ever
since that time evangelical groups have sought fulfillment of
some of the promises they believed were made in exchange for
their votes. This move finds sympathy in many quarters, for
who, even the irreligious, can claim to be against prayer. However, intrusion of such religious practice in public institutions
creates serious problems with the First Amendment. The pressure for prayer in public schools reflects the attempt by this
movement to resolve the problem of the erosion of communal
life through the recovery of traditional values.

Fundamentalist challenges to public education have not
stopped with school prayer. They have sought to control se-
lection of textbooks, and especially those dealing with biological evolution. The target of the attack has been the mythical
entity called "secular humanism." The real target has been any
teaching that seemed to contradict basic tenets of their confessional faith. This has included not only evolutionary theory but

also sexual education and many classical texts that seemed to reflect a nontraditional lifestyle. The struggle over evolution has changed somewhat since the trial of John Scopes in 1925. In recent years the fundamentalist approach has been to request a place for "scientific creationism" along with evolution. The hope is that introduction of God-talk in the discussion of creation would permit a theory of origins more in line with evangelical faith. This has been a bitter struggle and one that has been damaging not only to students but also to the evangelical communities.

Creationist thinking rests upon a popular view of science that has been dominant in the West for centuries, although it was discarded long ago by sophisticated science. In this view, truth is contained in facts which are brute data, unaltered by human thinking or observation. Thus, science was supposed to get at truth by getting to these brute facts. Whatever was true was given by the facts, and everything else was fantasy or wishful thinking. Taking this popular scientism for granted, fundamentalism assumed that biblical materials must contain irrefutable facts or they could not be true accounts of the relationship of God to human life and history. Two events in the nineteenth century exacerbated this situation for evangelical faith. Historical method came under the spell of this factual view of truth and began a methodical search of biblical materials. The net result was a challenge to the factual historicity of events such as the parting of the Red Sea and the historical life of Jesus. At the same time, Charles Darwin's work on the origin of species raised serious questions about the factual historicity of the creation stories in the Scriptures. With these two events, the lines of battle were drawn between fundamentalism and the empirical sciences.

It is important to recognize that fundamentalism was unconsciously pursuing a scientific approach in its claim to absolute, factual data in the Scriptures. They accepted the popular scientific view of truth as fact and applied it to their faith. Meanwhile, the sciences broke away slowly from this naive realism, recognizing that their theories were hypotheses to be tested yet always open to question. Newtonian physics gave way to the relativity theory of Einstein and cosmic theories went through radical changes. It soon became obvious that science was a human exploration in which new theories were constantly being tried and tested without discrediting the scientific enterprise. Meanwhile, historians began to recognize the diversity of perspectives within which historical documents could be viewed. A less arrogant history began to emerge, evincing much more appreciation for the diversity of cultures and their perspectives on reality. For many this meant the recognition that the cosmos could not be encompassed by concepts and categories, however useful they might be for science. Poetic, artistic, narrative, and symbolic forms gave much more access to these depths and heights of human life.

The fundamentalist approach, however well intentioned, has missed the opportunity of allying itself with the new science and historical inquiry. In claiming an absolute, infallible Scripture, fundamentalists have closed off these rich resources for appreciating the profound religious experience that is recorded in the Scriptures. At the same time, they have cut their young people off from modern science, at least as it relates to these realms of faith. The net effect has been to transform the biblical materials into law codes, turning poetry into pseudoscience. The impoverishment of evangelical faith is the result of this confusion of biblical truth with a popular science of facts. However, the resistance to science has played an important symbolic role in fundamentalist communalism. Science is the foremost symbol of modernity, the core of the challenge of the high-tech society to traditional values. Evangelical challenge to evolutionary theory and secular humanism has been above all a turning away from the forces of modernity which have eroded older values.

Perhaps the most dismaying element in the fundamentalist pursuit of communal values is their entertainment of the threat of Armageddon. This final battle between good and evil is presumably foretold in the Book of Revelation. The claim is that all the wicked forces will be destroyed in a final holocaust which is to be brought about by God. This traditional theme of the Last Days is distorted in contemporary fundamentalism and applied to a nuclear war between the superpowers. This human process of destruction is thus rationalized as a divine work. Consequently, amassing nuclear weapons is considered a virtuous work. A. G. Motjabai has set forth this evangelical view in her study of Amarillo, Texas, *Blessed Assurance: At Home with the Bomb in Amarillo, Texas.* In a sympathetic study, she shows how the acceptance of Armageddon has made many people in this community comfortable with the local Pantex Corporation, which assembles nuclear weapons for the United States government.

Another aspect of this doctrine of the Last Things is the theme of rapture. According to this interpretation, the saints or believers will be spared the holocaust. They will be taken up to heaven just before the destruction begins. As Jerry Falwell pointed out in a sermon, Christians will be riding in a car with others, and the Christians will disappear, leaving the car driverless on the highway. This is not a comforting thought, nor is it intended to be. But here again, communal values are affirmed in that believers will be saved and their enemies will be destroyed.

Such views can remove any serious concern with the threats of nuclear destruction. In fairness to the fundamentalist perspective, there *are* biblical passages that lend credence to such ideas if they are taken literally or out of context. On the other hand, the churches in the first few centuries had to come to terms with the reality that the world was not ending and was to be their home.

Fundamentalism is not by any means limited to confessional communities. In fact, commitment to national security is much the most important expression of fundamentalism in many parts of the world. National security is now invoked in most modern states as sufficient justification for military escalation and pursuit of proxy wars. This is the fundamentalism of national religion. At the same time, it is crucial to be aware of the broader implications of these movements. The technical society has eroded personal and communal bonds. It has undermined social order by its imperative of accumulation, success, and self-advancement. Further, the evangelical grasp at absolutes reflects a crisis in theological understanding, a failure by faith communities to come to terms with modern science and historical research. Nationalist and confessional fundamentalisms are driven by a nostalgia for a way of life long past. There are many values to be preserved from that way of life, but they cannot be sustained without incorporating them in the emerging world. Moreover, that new world is a global community of many faiths and peoples. Fundamentalism in national or confessional forms obscures that larger world in which all peoples now share. We are living in a world of pluralistic faiths and postcolonial peoples who are claiming their right to be subjects of their own histories. Yet Western Christianity, in most of its forms, continues to think in terms of the conversion of the world to the Christian faith. To this extent, religious institutions are lending their support to Western imperialism. This is true of most confessional bodies, although it is proclaimed more vigorously by the evangelical groups.

Fundamentalism brings these and other issues to the forefront in any consideration of the contemporary search for new, communal forms. To the extent that this search has a spiritual center, global trends to various forms of fundamentalism will have to be faced and challenged. At the same time, the concern of these movements for basic moral and spiritual values deserves to be taken seriously in any struggle for societal transformation.

Private Communalism

From Alexis De Tocqueville's visit in the early nineteenth century to the present, observers have commented on the individualistic character of American life. The individual orientation goes back even further in the British tradition, to the writings of Thomas Hobbes. After his publication of *Leviathan*, it became more and more common to take the individual as the ultimate entity in moral and political philosophy. David Hume, John Locke, John Stuart Mill, and many others followed in this tradition. This orientation was likewise the foundation for classical economic theory, so that David Ricardo and Adam Smith could take it for granted. Mercantile capitalism and later industrial development built upon the individual's market relationships as the accepted pattern for economic contracts and negotiations. Even the corporation was later legally recognized as an individual or corporate person.

An individualistic interpretation of the American experience is so conventional that one wonders whether it should be mistrusted. Yet today's individualism is not the individualism of the American frontier. It is a privatized individualism that has its counterpart in the private salvation of souls in the fundamentalist movement. Corporate capitalism in the twentieth century holds little resemblance to the entrepreneurial division of labor that Adam Smith celebrated. It is organized in large bureaucratic structures. It actually extends across national boundaries, often taking the form of transnational corporations. Except for a few individuals who hold top positions, work in corporate life is anything but a matter of individual decisions. Those who can find a place in the system are given considerable security and a reasonable income. The only condition is that they subordinate their lives to the corporate system. Those who fall into the secondary labor market pursue a marginal existence of part-time work at low wages and periodic unemployment. Those who fall below this level flounder in a safety net that is actually full of holes. The story is the same in educational and governmental structures. This, then, is a strange paradox: Americans celebrate their individualism, yet they spend most of their working hours within corporate life.

Whatever the character of public life, there is considerable evidence that Americans cherish their individual freedom, putting an almost ultimate value upon it. Every year enormous numbers leave their jobs for self-employment. Studies of working-class Americans indicate that they value most highly those jobs and professions that allow for a maximum of individual autonomy in allocation of time. Even poorly paid professors and teachers are valued above corporate managers. Since very few can really make a living outside the corporate structures, individualism is fulfilled in American life through private life-styles. This is the meaning of freedom for most people today: personal values can only be achieved by paying one's dues to the corporate world. If one can gear into the system, one is assured of a reasonable life-style as a consumer. If one does well, it is possible to achieve a "yuppie" life-style. Individualism, then, is privatized on the American scene today, since it has little place in the public world of institutions. Nevertheless, there is a basic harmony between the private style of life and the operation of the massive bureaucracies. Both are committed to accumulating money and capital. Both are devoted to possessions, making this essentially an acquisitive society. However, the private style of life is pursued with a profound nostalgia for communal values, especially since the human is essentially a communal being. These communal values are sought in support groups, communal activism, local political concerns, and even in corporate life. However, they are centered in personal interests and fail to deal with the basic structures that are eroding communal solidarity.

It is fair to ask whether it is legitimate to use the term *religious* to describe these movements of private communalism. Why treat privatized individualism as a religious phenomenon? At least with much of fundamentalism, one can make a case that it has religious roots. However, individualism is just the way things are in this society. On the other hand, one can ask what other value holds ultimate worth for most Americans. Even institutional religious life is lived out as an individual enterprise. The religious person is actually the major topic in most American sermons; in fact, the confessional communities have been a major support structure for individualism, placing decisive value on individual experience and profession of faith.

An argument for treating private communalism as a sacred endeavor can be drawn from a recent critical study of individualism in America. Robert Bellah and his associates in *Habits of the Heart* are critical of the forms that individualism has taken and of its limitations in dealing with the public responsibilities of citizenship. Nonetheless, they are basically in accord with the valuation of the individual in this tradition. Despite their critical concern, the following paragraph indicates the degree to which they, too, accept the individual as the sacred reality:

> Individualism lies at the very core of American culture. Every one of the four traditions we have singled out is in a profound sense individualistic. There is a biblical individualism and a civic individualism as well as a utilitarian and an expressive individualism. Whatever the differences among the traditions and the consequent differences in their understandings of individualism, there are some things they all share, things that are basic to American identity. We believe in the dignity, indeed the sacredness, of the individual. Anything that would violate our right to think for ourselves, judge for ourselves, make our own decisions, live our lives as we see fit, is not only morally wrong, it is sacrilegious. Our highest and noblest aspirations, not only for our-

selves, but for those we care about, for our society and for the world, are closely linked to our individualism. Yet, as we have been suggesting repeatedly in this book, some of our deepest problems both as individuals and as a society are also closely linked to our individualism. We do not argue that Americans should abandon individualism—that would mean for us to abandon our deepest identity. But individualism has come to mean so many things and to contain such contradictions and paradoxes that even to defend it requires that we analyze it critically, that we consider especially those tendencies that would destroy it from within.[2]

The authors might feel that they were speaking carelessly in using such religious language in their defense of individualism, but the book is carefully developed and these remarks are utterly serious. And, indeed, the sentiments in this quotation are repeated again and again in the interviews which the team conducted. Some of those whom they interviewed followed what they call "utilitarian individualism," which is essentially pursuit of success and personal interests. Others were more concerned with their feelings and inner states, pursuing their salvation in therapy groups or intimate communities. Whatever the path of fulfillment or salvation, the prime value was personal autonomy. Several decades ago, Thomas Luckmann published a short volume titled, *The Invisible Religion*, in which he argued that the individual was the sacred reality of American life today. In many ways, the text by Bellah and his associates confirms that judgment. The real question, then, is whether this is an adequate religious reality to undergird the American future.

The authors of *Habits of the Heart* believe that individualism alone is not an adequate basis on which to resolve the problems of the Western world. Their main argument is twofold. They believe that this radical individualism makes it impossible for Americans to understand the corporate world that determines so much of their lives. We are familiar with this phenomenon in recent presidential elections, where candidates run as opponents of big government; once in office, the bureaucracies continue to grow and the incumbents become superbureaucrats. Their other argument is that the American individual ends up as an isolated entity, unable to account for his or her deepest commitments and intimacies. This second dynamic, the inadequacy of radical individualism for a communal being, creates the search for community within a private world.

One of the striking facts about radical individualism is that it creates a gnawing hunger for community while eroding the very communities that might have sustained it. One cannot pursue private interests as a total way of life without undermining even the most intimate communities. Some of the communities that have emerged from this desperate search have been pathological. Innumerable cults and movements have been spawned by this passion for community. Private interests in individual or group form do not provide an adequate base for dealing with massive government and corporate structures. Even the public issues that can be pursued are embraced in fragmented ways.

Individualism and fundamentalism are two sides of the same coin. Both seek fulfillment of life and hope in the private realm of personal life, surrendering the public world to corporate, bureaucratic institutions. Nevertheless, both reveal a profound longing for personal community. Studies such as *Hidden Injuries of Social Class*, by Richard Sennett and Jonathan Cobb, bear out the high priority of community within radical individualism. However, there is no inner basis of community in either fundamentalism or radical individualism. A marriage or community built on self-interest begins to dissolve when one's interests change or are disappointed. In a different way, fundamentalist community lacks an inner ground for community; its only basis is an external, authoritative "word" or charismatic leader. To take an extreme case, Jim Jones tells the people at Jonestown when they are to commit suicide, whether they wish it or not, and they march to death at gunpoint. Every lasting community rests ultimately upon internal bonds of loving and caring, while preserving personal choice and freedom. Neither fundamentalism nor radical individualism furnishes such bonding and freedom. Fundamentalism depends upon external authority. Radical individualism depends upon a personal autonomy that is finally inimical to communal life. In both cases, the longing for community is undermined even as it is being pursued.

The worth of the person is one of the important values that has emerged in Western life. Whatever course is followed in the Western crisis, it will be crucial to preserve this value, as Bellah and his associates argue. However, the basic question is how the person (the so-called individual) is connected with the human community. So long as the individual is treated as an isolated entity, surviving on his or her own, societies will oscillate between fragmented individualism and collectivism. This has been the tragic reality of the twentieth century. Until person and community become integral to the organization of society, there will be no escape from these painful oscillations.

The unanswered question in Western liberalism is why community is so important to so many people, if, as the tradition claims, the individual is the ultimate entity. The same argument holds against the traditional view of God as absolute and sole: On what basis could a creation be meaningful to such an insulated deity? In fact, a case could be made that modern individualism is only a projection on the human scene of the imagery of autonomous deity. One could argue, against this tradition, that the hunger for community reveals a communal dimension of the human being and of the Divine Mystery as well. The basic fault in Western individualism is that it lacks a foundation for communal sensibility beyond the usefulness of others to the egoistic self. The communal movements emerging throughout the world are challenging this distortion of the nature of human life.

Public Communalism

The communal movement gained prominence in the nineteenth century. It blossomed as a protest against the fragmentation of life in Western society. Martin Buber is perhaps the best known of those who argued against the radical individualism of the West. However, there are many others, including John MacMurray in England, Emmanuel Mounier in France, John Dewey in the United States, and more recently such writers as Roberto Unger, Richard Bernstein, Alisdair MacIntyre, and the team that has worked with Robert Bellah. None of these figures is a proponent of any kind of collectivism. Their critique is primarily addressed to the exaggerated stress on the isolated individual in Western liberalism. Here the term "liberalism" does not refer to politically liberal thought but to the commercial view of society as a "free" market of competing, isolated individuals.

Although the origins are not always obvious, these figures in the communal movement had their roots in communities that fostered an entirely different life-style. This was especially true of Martin Buber's roots in the Hasidic movement. John Dewey found his real home in the educational communities that he did so much to establish. England has long had communal movements going back to figures such as Charles Kingsley and Frederick Dennison Maurice. Mounier was associated throughout his life with a personalist movement and published the journal *Esprit* in that context. This personalism was social through and through. Then, of course, there was Karl Marx, who held a thoroughly social, communal view of human nature. No matter how much some forms of later Marxism degenerated into collectivism, and this may have been fate in the fragmented Industrial Age, Marx's basic understanding centered on personal freedom and communal solidarity.

Our present concern, however, can best be served by looking at the contemporary struggles for community. These are diffuse and varied, but there are some common elements that can be identified. Even an all-too-brief look at some of these movements can provide clues to the direction of this struggle to overcome the crisis of Western life.

One of the most significant, communal movements in North America in recent years is the blacks' struggle for rights. This is, of course, an ancient struggle that began with the arrival of the first slave ships. Over the last few centuries it has gone through many phases, from slave revolts to the Garveyites; however, its recent flowering came in the late 1950s and 1960s with the struggle for civil rights. Martin Luther King, Jr., who made such a heroic contribution to this struggle and to the whole life of the United States, continues to be the central figure in this movement, though many of those who shared in the conflicts are now important actors in American political life. This is a long-term struggle, for racism continues to be a serious problem in American life.

Certain features of the recent civil rights movement shed light on the character of public communalism. The black struggle has drawn vitality from the deeply rooted religious life of black people, a religious dynamic going back to the days of slavery and continuing to this day. Unlike the white confessional bodies, the black churches always maintained a close tie with the economic and political struggle of black people to survive in racist America. It is no accident that the leading figure of the rights struggle was a religious leader of remarkable stature who held together the personal and public concerns of his people. Those who participated in the movement recall vividly the services of worship, which were prayerful yet functioned as rallies to carry the community forward into dangerous conflicts. This bonding of personal and public in black confessional religion continues to be its special power as a communal force.

The recent rights movement, and undoubtedly many that preceded it, brought an important awareness of the dignity and worth of black people, challenging the racism to which they were subjected. This communal sense of black worth continues to further the black cause in America. Furthermore, the poverty and suffering of black people in the United States, consequent upon generations of discrimination, means that the black struggle remains the touchstone of all social struggles in this country. The sure test of any remedy for unemployment, welfare dependency, homelessness, or poverty is to ask how it will affect the black community. This gives the black struggle first place as a benchmark in any attempt to confront the social ills of the West, and of the United States in particular. This black priority is not exclusive of other communal movements, such as the plight of Hispanic peoples, American Indians, handicapped persons, and other minorities. In each instance, the touchstone of policy is the plight of the oppressed and suffering.

Another public communal movement of great importance in the United States is the women's movement or movements. It is a highly diverse phenomenon embracing radical feminism, a rights struggle, and a more general concern for liberation from many of the constraints and inequalities that have oppressed women throughout history. One of its important accomplishments has been the creation of a sense of solidarity among women, although this has also pitted the women's movement against more conservative groups. Moreover, it has opened new horizons for women in work, political life, institutional religion, and artistic fields. Its most difficult struggle has been discrimination in jobs and wages. The campaign for the Equal Rights Amendment was an attempt to gain sound legal footing for challenging the many forms of discrimination that women experience in American life. One of the most pressing problems the movement will be facing is the feminization of poverty in American society. Women and children now comprise over two-thirds of the impoverished people in our urban areas. This places the women's movement close to the black struggle as a benchmark for solutions to our social issues.

On the face of it, there does not seem to be a religious dimension to the women's movement, except in the most general sense. In reality it is a profoundly religious struggle against one of the most deeply rooted, Western religious prejudices—the patriarchal image of the Divine Mystery. This image of divinity has undergirded the hierarchical domination of bureaucratic life as well as the sexism that pervades all aspects of American life. The symbolism of Divine Life in the Western traditions is paternalistic, authoritative, and hierarchical. It allows little place for democratic process and even less for the place of women. Patriarchalism may well account for the intense resistance to the women's movement and to the Equal Rights Amendment by more traditional confessional bodies. Insofar as the women's movement succeeds in transforming the patriarchalism of Western society, it will initiate a religious reformation of fundamental dimensions. This places the women's movement in the forefront of the search for a more humane cosmology. It could reshape the direction of Western society, possibly toward more democratic practices in working and governing. Such an outcome of the women's movement is quite independent of any specific connection of the movement with institutional religious life, although the feminist struggle has had strong proponents within mainline confessional bodies.

The grassroots Christian communities of South and Central America constitute another movement of great importance to the Western future. They have spearheaded the struggle for justice in many Latin American countries, playing such an important role that they have been the specific target of attacks by the United States, in particular by the CIA. The Santa Fe document promulgated by the transition team of the Reagan administration was directed against the Catholic church of Latin America because of its influence in this communal movement. The movement emerged out of work with the poor by priests, lay catechists, and nuns. After three centuries of almost total identification with the rich establishment, the church had begun to show a new and vital concern for the poor. The response was spontaneous and widespread. In time there were roughly eighty thousand grassroots communities in Brazil alone.

It would seem that this is, after all, just one more expression of institutional religion. However, the movement is a radical departure in the Catholic tradition—a people's church, as Pope John Paul II called it on his visit to Central America. It represents an attempt to thrust the work of confessional communities into the heart of the political and economic struggle for a just society. Hence, it is essentially a lay movement, although supported by religious leadership. It may well be a sign of the new expression of confessional life, a full commitment to public communalism. It is significant that the pastoral letter on the United States economy of the National Conference of Catholic Bishops took the commitment to the poor of these grassroots communities as the guiding principle of its proposals.

One other movement can be mentioned, although it is a complex global phenomenon that cannot be reduced to a single process. This is the peace movement, which has resisted the proliferation of nuclear weapons and the militarization of the globe. It is estimated that in 1986 eight hundred billion dollars was spent on armaments in a world plagued by hunger and malnutrition. Again, one might say that the peace movement reveals little in the way of religious orientation, although confessional bodies have been important participants. Yet "peace" is without doubt the most important single symbol of religious life in the West. The word *Shalom* is central to the Jewish and Muslim traditions. Jesus is often referred to in the Christian tradition as the Prince of Peace. The triumph of Islam is intended to bring a reign of peace. If there is any symbol that embodies the religious hopes of peoples throughout the world, it is the symbol of peace. The centrality of this symbol in contemporary movements reveals the shift in the religious center of gravity from confessional bodies to a public communalism. The hope in this movement is that national security may become people's security; this is, at least, the finding of Zsuza Hegedus in her article "The Challenge of the Peace Movement: Civilian Security and Civilian Emancipation."[3]

The communal movements mark an important advance in the search for a spiritual center and community of peoples. The deeper hungers in fundamentalist and private communalism, their concerns for moral values, can be realized only in public movements. However, the question remains as to the foundations of communalism. A lack of grounding became evident in a theological experiment in the 1970s: "Theology of the Americas," a movement which sought to incorporate the experience of the Latin American grassroots communities into the North American struggle for justice, failed despite some good things that emerged from it. Following the American pattern of pursuing the individual's or group's special interests, black, women's, Asian, Hispanic, and other caucuses transformed the movement into an aggregation of interest groups. This is the collective expression of private communalism that is characteristic of a market society. Such interests have a legitimate place in political process, but centering community in interest groups undermines any attempt to achieve some common ground or basic commitments. The important point is that the ground for personal and communal life is far from clear. Moreover, the ideologies of free markets and collective control have lost both their appeal and viability. This lack of grounding for community is as true of confessional bodies today as it is of the broader religious struggle over public values in the West.

The confessional bodies have an important contribution to make to the resolution of the crisis of public religious values. They are rooted in communal traditions, even though their faith interpretations have been conditioned by Western individualism. We have seen the impact of black communalism on the civil rights struggle. The grassroots communities of Latin America also demonstrate the influence of the communal roots of the Catholic heritage. However, these contributions are possible only where the confessional communities recover their own communal roots. Certain religious values of the possessive society may well be preserved and transformed under this communal influence. For example, a humane work-place, productivity, personal choice, and opportunity are all important to a healthy community; however, even these central values in the present society are being undermined by individualism and the bureaucratic domination that organizes it.

By contrast, the technical transformation of the modern world has brought people into close juxtaposition and provides the means for communication and communal solidarity. However, technology is mobilized at present largely in the struggle for resources and markets. Unfolding the communal nature of human life does not of itself resolve these macroproblems, but it does set the stage for seeing new possibilities amid our present difficulties. Only in this way can a foundation be laid for a creative resolution of the crisis of public faith that now undermines the future of high-tech societies. Since this technical spirit has gained hegemony throughout the world, the future of the peoples of many faiths and cultures will depend upon such a communal transformation of the possessive societies.

Chapter Two
The Web of Life

Despite a nostalgia for community, individualism yields slowly to the reawakening of communal sensibilities. Patterns of competitive achievement in school and work reinforce a sense of autonomy. Political rhetoric refers to welfare services as a "safety net," portraying each person as a tightrope walker perched far above the ground. This image distorts the communal being of persons and numbs society to the suffering of its members. The paradox of this orientation is that it also undermines the person as an individual. The person who cannot walk the tightrope is categorized as a failure. Those who manage to stay aloft are treated as expendable means for the working of the system. (Needless to say, the net is full of holes.) The tragedy of the individualistic heritage is that its suppression of communal dimensions has destroyed the individual value which it purported to honor. A distortion of communal being results in extreme swings from private individualism to collective, mass society. The rhetoric of individualism perpetuates the hunger of persons for communal supports while crippling efforts for public communal healing.

We are concerned with community building of a kind that cherishes the liberties of persons. The communal way of being is the very heart of personal life. Where it emerges in local and public forms, persons are treated with respect, their voices are heard. We shall attempt in this chapter to disclose the interpersonal way of being by considering a difficult personal question, the decision for or against abortion. We open our reflections with this controversial issue because the depths of personal being are only revealed in the most difficult situations.

The Debate: Pro-Birth versus Pro-Choice

Preoccupation with fetal life is a recent phenomenon in the Western world. Many factors may have contributed to this concern, including widespread awareness of the threat of nuclear annihilation. In many ways this intense concern with fetal life contrasts dramatically with public disregard for prenatal and postnatal care among the poor, at least on the part of conservative groups. The Reagan administration caused an increase in infant mortality from 1980 to 1986 through cuts in programs for prenatal care and food stamps. This placed the United States eighteenth among industrialized nations in infant mortality.[1] Meanwhile, the administration promoted legislation to overturn the 1973 decision of the Supreme Court on abortion rights. This is a case of protecting the right to birth while undermining the right to life. This contradiction between concern for fetal life and neglect of human life is a paradox that raises questions about the understanding of human life in this conflict.

There seems to be no disagreement between pro-choice and anti-choice groups over "respect for life." The main issue is whether fetal life is to be counted as "human" or "personal" life in the full sense. Furthermore, there is no real difference over respect for and protection of the fetus, though again the status of fetal life is interpreted very differently. Advocates of the rights of fetal life hold an individualistic view of the person, and thus, by analogy, of the fetus. Their argument is that the embryo or fetus is a discrete human being, quite apart from relations to the mother or with the larger community. To abort a fetus, then, is to terminate a human life. This view accords with Western individualism. The picture on the pro-choice side of the conflict is mixed. Some proponents of procreative choice persist in the individualistic tradition. Their main argument for woman's choice juxtaposes the rights of the prospective mother with rights of the fetus, treating each as discrete entities. On their side, they place the well-being of the mother first. However, others in the pro-choice movement hold a communal understanding of the person. They reject the claim that fetal life can be viewed as an independent entity.

Beverly Harrison illumines some of the personal issues surrounding fetal life among the groups involved in the conflict. Following the findings of modern embryology, she argues that the fetus is a form of human life. In fact, most groups involved in the conflict affirm continuity in life processes. The crucial issue is at what point in this life process a human being or person is presumed to exist. Granting this continuity, she observes:

> Even so, I believe it is inadmissible to predicate to a fetus at any given point in its development existent human functions that its actual degree of structural complexity cannot sustain. Analogies to us, I believe, are inappropriate if they attribute to a fetus autonomous and existent human life functions that its structural development could not support. Hence, to call a conceptus or an early differentiated fetus "a human being," or even "a person" is, in my view, genuinely absurd, because the actualized biological structure existent in early fetal development cannot conceivably manifest the qualities we impute to "a human being," much less to "a person." Such analogies limp because they leap a biological chasm that only rhetorical force can bridge.[2]

In pursuing this phase of her discussion, Dr. Harrison argues for the moment of birth as the point at which one would speak of human life. At the same time, she argues for respect for fetal life at every stage and especially in later phases of development.

The main argument of Harrison's text is that personal being, even in its postnatal stage, is a relational reality, dependent upon care and nurture in order to unfold. The fetus is dependent upon the nurture of the parent, and the neonate is dependent upon loving care in order to come to full personhood. Thus, she makes the case that personhood is a communal moral category which depends for its very being upon the qualities of the bonds in which it emerges and develops. Drawing on the work of Mary Anne Warren, she identifies some of the criteria of personhood, and then remarks:

> Even more strongly than Warren, I would argue that fetuses in late stages of development should be extended respect, not because they are persons but because they have arrived at the threshold of discrete biological existence as a human life form— the point where it makes the most sense to posit the existence of foundational requirements of personhood.[3]

Beverly Harrison adduces several arguments for women's right to procreative choice. One line of the argument is present in the passages that we have quoted, although this presentation cannot do justice to the full scope of her considerations. The main point is that the pregnant woman bears the burden of moral responsibility not only in carrying the fetus but in providing the nurture that is so crucial to the becoming of personhood. In this sense, she argues for a moral communal view of personal life. Whatever the decision on abortion, it would have to be settled on this level of interpersonal responsibilities.

Individual Rights versus Personal Relations

Carol Gilligan's studies of moral development do not deal directly with the debate over the moral justification of abortion; however, her work brings to light what is at stake in crucial decisions about human relationships. Procreation involves inescapable responsibility for life. After a lifetime of education in passivity and self-sacrifice, many women find it extremely difficult to work through a decision that may involve furthering their own well-being at the cost of fetal life. No amount of pro-and-con argument can ignore the agonies suffered by women in making such decisions. This is a caveat that is important to introduce, since my own concern is with the understanding of the person in such decisions. In many cases, women came to personal and moral maturity in making these decisions.

A basic issue in the conflict over procreative choice is the understanding of the person. Carol Gilligan opens up this question in terms of the moral development of men and women from adolescence to adulthood. She has challenged current theories of moral development, which have been constructed largely from men's experience. She introduces a counterpoint into this inquiry, drawing on women's experience. She does not cast her argument in terms of radical individualism versus a relational understanding of personal being, although this contrast is implicit in her studies. She formulates the difference in terms of male detachment and female attachment. These are not meant as biologically based terms. She does not seem to be arguing for an "essential" female way of being. The differences develop through cultural and social differences of life space.

Most studies of psychological development have been drawn from experiences of boys and men. This is as true of Piaget's pioneering work as of Erik Erikson's and Lawrence Kohlberg's work. In these studies, women appear as partially developed or morally immature. The main reason for this finding is that women are concerned about relationships, about harmonizing the web of relations in which they live. Men, on the other hand, stress individual achievement, success, fulfillment of their ambitions, and willingness to abide by the rules of the game in order to protect their own rights. Since moral theory has been explored primarily by male philosophers, it has followed a similar path, defining moral maturity in terms of objective, impersonal, and principled judgments. The basic notion underlying such theories is that a valid morality is detached from personal bonds, achieving universality through impartiality. The ideal moral agent is, thus, the detached, neutral observer. This view conforms to the male life trajectory in Western, technical society. The successful man presumably gains autonomy through achievements. Women appear deficient when the game is defined in this way, for they have been largely restricted to familial communities until recent years.

Kohlberg traces the logic of moral development from early concern with one's own needs to concern for community norms to detached and universal judgments. This is a continuous process of distancing, impersonality, and objectivity. It fits the analytic and technical order of a society built around contracts and market negotiations. Since interests are discrete and subjective in the market society, only commonly accepted rules can provide a framework for pursuit of business. The individual is viewed as a bundle of interests, connected to other individuals by reciprocal needs and rights. Carol Gilligan interprets this theory of rights and rules as a morality of justice. Men seem to operate in this way. She contrasts this with a morality of interpersonal relationships. She views the women's perspective as a morality of care, one in which the primary concern is to sustain and enrich the web of human relationships. These are not gender or biological distinctions, as we noted. They are culturally formed and transmitted, although women's reproductive role may well reinforce concern for relationships. The "rights and rules" approach is actually a truncated view of justice that will have to be reconstructed; for the moment, it may suffice to contrast these moralities as care versus justice.

Men who are culturally programmed to move toward autonomy in their life trajectories may, and often do, slide through parenthood and adult life without the kind of crisis that can awaken them to intimacy and care. To be sure, few men or women go through life without suffering acute crises of illness or broken relationships or failures so that life provides many transition points. However, both men and women begin life with personal intimacy, since care is a primordial experience in the growth of persons. In an article on care and justice, Gilligan noted that Piaget found in his original studies that boys as well as girls initially expressed empathy and care. The point of departure in life seems to be identical for men and women. Piaget dismissed this finding in his study, so it never bore fruit. This suggests that the male orientation to detached autonomy is created by suppression of emotional attachments.[4]

If care is this deeply rooted, and how else does the child come to be as a person except through the love and nurture of parents and/or siblings and/or relatives or other persons. Whether maturation to self-identity and intimacy occurs or not depends, undoubtedly, on circumstances, relationships, and the kinds of decisions that have shaped a person's life. In many cases, persons who have suffered distorting relationships achieve remarkable sensitivity and maturity in later years. At the same time, some persons become so estranged through their preoccupation with success and achievement that they seem to lose all touch with their feelings and with other persons. It is also striking, in this connection, that in almost all of the cases cited in this study of women deciding about abortion, the men involved—whether boyfriends, husbands, or lovers— had pressed the women to have abortions. The men did not want to be hampered with parenthood or with additional children. A society that cultivates male autonomy as a way of life can hardly be expected to produce men who put a high premium on care and responsibility for others.

We come to be as persons through the care of others, and we achieve our own moral maturity in learning to care for others as well as ourselves. This transition from selfish concern for ourselves to mutuality of care is a moral maturation in personal relationships. Yet the question remains as to how we are to understand this communal being of our personhood. Is it that we belong to one another? If this is so, we are inwardly bonded with one another and, thus, we are interpersonal, communal beings through and through. We can never erase that bonding, though it may be impoverished by life and relationships. We never lose the longing for intimacy and community, no matter how alienating our life experiences. We are essentially moral interpersonal beings. If we were only externally connected to one another, becoming communal merely through pursuit of our needs and interests, then we would be marginally communal and moral. However, granting the communal nature of persons, there remains the question of how persons become independent separate selves.

Persons in Community

The transition to moral adulthood illumines the communal reality of personal life. We discover who we are or can become through our bonding with others. This seems a rather obvious insight, yet, the conventional wisdom is that we are separate entities, coming to maturity through asserting our independence. We are first connected beings, inwardly bonded with one another. However, this communal reality of our being does not obstruct the emergence of personal identity and integrity; rather, it undergirds individuality through interpersonal affirmation of worth. If, as is the case with most men, we are socialized into radical separateness, then we can achieve moral maturity only through intimate experiences of love that renew our bondedness with others. If, as is often the case with women, we are socialized into dependency on men, then the path to full maturity involves coming to one's own separate identity as a person of worth. We are constituted by our relations. This is true of all reality. We dwell in a cosmos of interrelated, internally connected energies and processes, each event affecting and altering every other event, however slightly.

The communality of personhood is so obvious that the remarkable thing is that Western technical society was able to suppress it. We know that newborn infants can grow, learn to speak, and achieve a sense of self only through the love and care of parents or surrogates. When this physical and spiritual nurture is missing or deficient, and certainly it is never perfect, children are damaged and limited. Yet no matter how much this communal being of personal life is suppressed and distorted in technical society, the hunger for community persists, if only as nostalgia.

Several accounts of women making decisions about abortion trace the process of transition to moral maturity. Betty, a sixteen-year-old, was delayed in obtaining a second abortion by an abortion counselor at the clinic. Her first abortion had followed a rape while she was hitchhiking. The second abortion was demanded by her boyfriend. Betty had never come to terms with the fact that she was an adopted child. Her adolescence had been particularly turbulent. She had difficulty in school, became involved with drugs, and had difficulty with her parents. The counseling over the abortion decision provided Betty with a crucial occasion for transition in moral judgment. At first she had thought primarily of her personal survival, her freedom to do as she pleased, and her dependency on her boyfriend. She gradually came to terms with her responsibilities. She became aware of the importance of the future of the child she was bearing. She thought about the child's future with no father (the boyfriend had left), her lack of education, and a life mired in poverty. She made the decision in favor of the abortion after agonizing over her responsibilities. In the course of this struggle, she achieved a sense of her own self, of her debt to her adoptive parents, and of the course she would have to follow for a decent life. The decisive reality in her transformation was the dawning sense that the life within her had a possible future as a person in need of nurture and care. She came to realize that there was no way in which she could provide for this child, as much as she wanted the baby for her own comfort. In the projection of this possibility of responsibilities which she could not fulfill, she began to sense her own personhood and worth. She worked through to a new level of moral responsibility through the discovery of her bond with a fetal life for which she could not provide.

Carol Gilligan interviewed Betty and Sarah who made somewhat comparable transitions to adulthood and moral responsibility. In each of these stories, as Dr. Gilligan observes, awareness of the claims of another "person" to whom one is bonded, in this case the child to be, opened the way to discovery of the worth of the self. The fetal life, in each instance, came to be as the other "person" toward whom responsibility was owed. The transition to moral responsibility became possible through the building of a narrative of obligations with alternative futures. This narrative power to redescribe the future is a creative expression of human imagination, endowing persons with the capacity to change. As artistic, imaginative beings, we are able to project in language alternative possibilities that enable us to discover ourselves in relation to others. We do not have to suffer every possible misfortune. We can project possibilities and test them against the wisdom of others as well as the experience of family and friends. Often we need the help of others in reconstructing our stories in ways that deal realistically with the issues we face.

Our stories are bearers of our identities, as we noted above. Moreover, in sharing our stories, we reveal ourselves to one another, shaping and reshaping our relationships. When we encounter a new person, we become acquainted through sharing certain experiences. This is even truer in loving relationships, where we begin to share our stories more intimately. Times of grief and mourning are also moments for sharing stories and relating important events in the life of a brother or sister or parent. Narrative is a principal means of achieving coherence in life. It brings together the many bits and pieces into a kind of totality.

Stories give us some hold on who we are, yet we are not stories. We are flesh and blood organisms that feel pain as well as joy. By the same token, fetal life is not a child or person in any sense that we normally use those terms, yet the fetus functioned as "child" in the scenarios that Betty and Sarah fashioned in working through their decisions about abortion. If we

are bodies and not stories, how can narratives help us to find a
workable future? On one level, the answer to this question is
obvious. We are creatures of words and meanings. We dwell
with one another through linguistic symbols and gestures. Husband and wife decide when to leave a gathering by facial expressions and gestures; at least, they do so when they are on
good terms. Yet trees, garbage cans, children, and books are
not words but things and bodies. At the same time, things only
become things in our world through the words, phrases,
names, and sentences that make them part of our common
life. "Things," then, really are word-things in the human
world. Archaeologists discover this reality in their work when
they find things that lie totally outside their experience, things
whose functions and purposes are utterly alien to their world.
Even when they name these things for the purpose of classifi-
cation, they realize that they do not know what they are and
would not know how to incorporate them into the world they
understand.

Stories work as metaphors. They recount events, yet they
are not the actual events. They are images of those events in
narrative form. We usually speak of metaphors as tropes or
linguistic substitutions. They are, in fact, transformations in
the meanings of words through sentences that disclose new
meanings. We speak of a "ship of state" to convey a sense of
direction in the body politic, and "body politic" is itself a
metaphoric shift. We speak of a "melancholy moment," even
though we know that time is neither melancholy nor joyful in
itself. A similar process seems to occur as we bring things that
are not mind into meaning through words.

Words do not bring things into meaning through similarities
of sounds in things to the phonetic sounds of the words, since
different languages can use very different words and sounds
for the same things. How much similarity in sound and feeling
entered into the primordial emergence of languages we do not
know and probably cannot discover. However, we are aware
that our discourse brings a flow of energies, rhythms, and pul-
sations of the world around us into meanings that we can
share. The basic rhythms of human and natural life find expression in our mathematical formulas, artistic creations, sciences, and linguistic communication. Poetry is, perhaps, the

most vivid expression of this metaphoric power, creating moods, feelings, and depths of understanding through sounds and rhythms as well as the play of verbal meanings. This is a metaphoric process that creates a world of meanings from the biological and cosmic flow in which our lives are embedded. The illusions of idealism are created by identifying these verbal meanings with reality. The trap of materialism is to discount the transformative power of metaphoric, linguistic creation. In contrast to both of these interpretations, we dwell in a world that is linguistically forged and yet ever interwoven with the interplay of bodies, things, rhythms, and energies of life and cosmos. Our discourse and stories are similar to these rhythms of life, yet, as is true of all metaphors, different.

The metaphoric power of linguistic understanding and communication enables us to dwell between past and future, retaining our past experience in symbolized memories and projecting our possible futures in images and scenarios. In this way Betty, as we noted, was able to experience the fetal life within her as "a child to be born" and to be lived with through the years ahead. Fetal life that was not yet "child" entered the community as "child" through the metaphoric power of narrative. In this sense, narrative itself is a metaphoric process, creating possible events, characters, acts, and outcomes that are similar to everyday occurrences but are not those ordinary events. By projecting various scenarios, Betty was able to describe and redescribe possible futures, anticipating outcomes that would be threatening or workable. In this process, she also became aware of her moral responsibility to the "child to be," to herself, and to others.

Love and Justice

The metaphoric interpretation of interpersonal life sheds light on the connection between care and justice. As noted above, Carol Gilligan identifies two moralities, one of care and one of justice. She views them as complementary, one stressing the web of relations, the other focusing on individual rights. Her studies indicate that women in American culture tend to operate with a morality of care and relationships. Men, for the most part, seem to act in terms of rights and interests. In Gilligan's perspective, care preserves communal bonds amid in-

equalities. Justice, within her perspective, preserves freedom
and equality by attending to individual interests and rights.
The ideal situation, given the assumption of complementarity,
would be for women to achieve a mature sense of justice while
maintaining their concern for human relations; inversely, men
would ideally achieve a capacity for care while retaining their
sense of rights and equality.

The distinction between care and justice misses the term *love*
that is essential to all human relationships. Love is a central
symbol in the religious moral heritage of the West. It has
played a minor role in our modern moral philosophies, but
that is all the more reason to raise questions about the Western
tradition. It would be naive to assume that Western philosophy
was correct in playing down such an important symbol. Despite
her important insights into problems of Western sexist thinking on morality, Carol Gilligan seems to have accepted its
rather impersonal view of justice. The net effect is to weaken
her critique of this detached view of human relations. The following reconstruction of Gilligan's insights is an attempt to
strengthen her position rather than to undermine it. A crucial
point in this revision is clarifying the place of love in the interplay of care and justice. One solution is simply to identify care
with love, assuming that caring for others is loving them. Since
love is such a comprehensive symbol, including much that we
call "care" and yet extending far beyond it, we shall be on better ground to recognize caring as an expression of love. This
fits our ordinary language, for we speak of caring about the
poor or caring for our parents as expressions of loving concern. This understanding of care as an aspect of loving actually
appears again and again in Gilligan's interviews.

The transition points for women deciding about abortion involved, as we have seen, becoming aware of their bonds with
the life within them, with their parents, husbands, boyfriends,
and the larger community. They experienced the agony of deciding about the future of fetal life, because they were profoundly conscious of their bonds with this life. This is the
experience of care in its deepest sense, care as being bonded in
love and concern. We have considered this inward bondedness
in the experiences of transformation that accompanied these
decisions. The pregnant woman is not only bonded with the

life within her but also with all those to whom she is connected in the web of life. We also acknowledged this bonding in the nurture of children; without such care, personal development is seriously hampered. However, loving care extends also to past experiences; in the case of these decisions about abortion, care meant coming to terms with one's own actions in the past, including responsibility for the pregnancy. This brings to light a symbol that is at the heart of loving care—the symbol of concern. As the decisions became more pressing, concern for their own past and the future of their "children" became paramount. What would the future hold for this "child to be born"? On another level, they were also posing questions about their own identities as persons. What did this decision mean for their being as persons? These moral questions are also religious questions. They pose ultimate issues of what it means to be a person, to be someone of worth who can live with self-respect. This is the level of concern that binds us to the things around us, to other persons, and to the very meaning of our lives. In this sense, the decisions about abortion brought to light practical issues of survival, moral questions of responsibility, and ultimate questions of the meaning of one's very being as a person.

Concern is a comprehensive symbol, which means that it includes the whole of our way of being with things, with other persons and amid the meanings that fill our lives. The religious community of Friends have long used the term *concern* to express a matter about which they had strong feelings and commitment. We are beings of concern, beings who are involved in things, engaged with our survival, and enmeshed in our relationships and in the myriad activities that fill our days. Concern, in this large sense, undergirds both love and justice, for it directs all of our relationships. Love and justice are the practical unfolding of concern in our relationships and activities.

We can grasp the comprehensive meaning of concern by locating it within the narrative framework which the women who were interviewed adopted in their decisions. Stories are crucial in human understanding because they can encompass a complex web of relations, both practical and spiritual. Stories weave together the various threads that tie us to our past and our future as well as to one another. Stories also disclose the circumstances that constrain us and/or advance our projects. Stories are, in this sense, portrayals of the working of concern in founding and shaping our world. They are also disclosure points in our lives, especially where our experiences have been damaging, whether by our own doing or that of others. This is one of the truths and great values of therapy in the rebuilding of personal lives. It is the opportunity to work through our stories and share them with others who manifest concern for us. We have noted the lack of concern by so many men in relation to the women who were facing decisions about pregnancy; their unwillingness to assume what Erik Erikson called generativity or responsibility toward the next generation. The women were also dealing with their own lack of concern in becoming pregnant, for in some cases it was a selfish or thoughtless step. Concern, then, is much more than a sentiment, mood, or attitude, though many moods, like sympathy, caring, and empathy are rooted in concern.

Concern is our way of being human, through our bonding to others, to ourselves, to our own stories, and to the circumstances of our lives. In this sense, concern opens out upon the questions of meaning and hope that shape our futures. Thus, concern guides and directs our bonding with other persons, with our work and activities, and with the larger meanings that make sense of our lives. This is not to suggest that we live daily in the right relations of concern, for we are constantly inclined to attend to our own desires, passions, and interests, overlooking the pains of those around us and even ignoring the needs of those close to us. However, such selfish inattention to human needs troubles us; we find ourselves trying to justify our actions, attempting to fit them into a moral framework that can prove to ourselves that we are not immoral or unworthy persons. Similarly, the nostalgia for community which we noted among autonomous individuals reveals the traces of earlier bonds.

Love creates and sustains the bonds of concern between persons. It manifests itself as caring in intimate relationships, and especially in the nurturing relations that we have been exploring. Love, as we shall see subsequently, is also the healing and rebuilding of broken relationships. This is its creative power as an expression of concern. Love also binds us to the higher values and meanings of life, both moral and spiritual. Love can be impoverished by a certain style of life, as we have seen in the case of men who are groomed for bureaucratic life. Love can also be impoverished in women who are groomed for personal popularity but not for assuming responsibility. However, concern is so fundamental to life that its impulses are retained and express themselves as longing for intimacy, community, and a life that is worthy of respect.

The practice of love unfolds concern not only for others but also for one's own being and worth. Communal bonding weaves a moral web that sustains our ties with one another and our affirmation of ourselves. These are the two sides of concern that love cultivates in a maturing personal life.

Justice is also grounded in concern, as we indicated. Justice and love are actually much closer together than our philosophical and theological traditions have acknowledged. Love is often treated as sacrificial and uninterested, while justice is reduced to rules and principles that advance interests and rights. We usually hear of justice as rendering to each his or her due, meaning by this a balancing of interests according to the set of values that are current in a society. In a competitive, achievement-oriented society like ours, one is rewarded according to abilities and accomplishments. However, justice has a more profound meaning. This is justice as right relations, an understanding that is basic to the biblical tradition. This is justice as the mutuality of shared being that arises from our bonding with one another, from our belonging to one another.[5] Thus, the churches taught for centuries that stealing food for one's starving family is morally justified, if no other alternative is open. Justice, in this sense, has to do with the very nature of things, their moral and spiritual worth, the right relations that are to prevail among them. The community's responsibility to share its food takes priority over individual claims to possession. This has to do with the being of persons and their worth.

Justice gives social and public form to concern. We shall have to explore this deeper meaning subsequently, but, for the moment, this gives some indication of why love and justice were so closely interwoven in the religious traditions of the West. The ultimate concern for the meaning of life itself and for the purpose of our own lives is the substance of the religious life, as Paul Tillich pointed out many years ago. Such ultimate concern may be repressed, as Mircea Eliade argued that it has been repressed in the modern world, but the concern does not disappear, since it is at the very foundation of our being. In this respect, the love and justice that flow from our deepest concern with our very being continue as beacons even amid the cruelest injustice and evil. We are also aware of this tie between love and justice in everyday affairs, for we seek justice for those we love. We are angered when those for whom we care are mistreated. So far as we have matured to a full humanity, we are angered at all injustice, for it violates the mutuality that constitutes our very being as human. Love seeks justice, even as justice brings love to fruition in mutually supportive relationships.

Nevertheless, there is tension between love and justice, for love strives to preserve the bonds of life, resisting the pressures to set some rights over others. It is the nature of most moral decisions that some values have to be given preference over others, lesser evils have to be chosen over greater evils. As we have seen in the cases of the women in Gilligan's study who were deciding about abortion, they had to gain a sense of their own worth, for they had grown up thinking that loving meant sacrificing their whole lives for others. Such sacrifice may be called for at times, but a person who feels no sense of worth has very little to sacrifice. Love for oneself involves rendering oneself justice, just as loving another means seeking justice for that person. The agony of many of these decisions for the women came from the reality that justice toward themselves and the future meant sacrificing their love for the "child" that they might have brought to term. Whether they made the best decisions cannot be judged from the outside, for they were caught in the tensions of love and justice, seeking a way that could bring a viable future under difficult circumstances. Their decisions, like all moral judgments, were metaphoric disclosures of the tensive interplay of competing goods or competing evils, judgments in which the tensive interplay of love and justice had to be resolved. A moral decision to bring the fetus to term involved the judgment that the just action was to give precedence to love for the "child to be," taking justice toward oneself and one's future relationships as truly expressed in this action. The decision to go through with the abortion gave precedence to justice toward oneself and one's future, bringing the fetus to term would be unjust to its future and unloving; thus, justice takes precedence and transforms the meaning of love. This is the metaphoric transformation of meaning that enters into moral decisions. Love and justice are similar, in that each seeks to maintain the mutuality of life; yet, they are different, for love seeks mutuality by preserving the web of life, while justice seeks mutuality by preserving the priorities in needs and rights. Laws and institutions, when they are true to the being of persons and communities, sustain the mutuality of life through right relations; however, they can never be a substitute for the personal and corporate decisions that adjudicate in particular cases. Love and justice are always in tension, and every resolution of the tension in the metaphoric judgment for one or the other attempts to unite them as an expression of concern.

This tensive interplay of love and justice reveals the metaphoric character of moral judgments. Love is like justice in seeking the well-being of the other, in this case the fetal life. Love is also different from justice, in that love seeks to preserve and maintain the web of life; however, justice presses the question of concern for the whole network of relations and persons, including the being of the pregnant woman. Choices had to be made, some needs had to be given priority over others. Love and justice come to a metaphoric resolution in which one or the other gains priority, yet both are fulfilled as concern in the true moral judgment. Some of the women in the study decided to bear their fetuses to term. Others decided to terminate the pregnancy and work for a better life. In bearing the children, some of the women let justice toward the fetal life take precedence over the bonds of love with lovers or husbands. Others who terminated the pregnancy let justice toward themselves take precedence over their love for the "child" whom they might have borne. These tensive resolutions cannot be reduced to a formula. They are expressions of concern, where the decisions are thoughtful and mature. They seek to preserve and heal the bonds of communal life and personal being so far as possible.

Formulas or laws are universal and abstract. They provide useful boundaries in reflecting on moral issues, but they cannot resolve the concrete issues of personal lives and circumstances. This is the reason why federal and state laws forbidding abortion become damaging to the community and to the very persons, including "children" that might be born, whom they are meant to protect. It is, of course, true that those who consider fetal life already human have grounds to claim that abortion comes under the rubric of killing. However, we have given reasons to suggest that this is an extreme judgment with little warrant in the realities of communal relations. Nevertheless, it can be said that laws have an important function in protecting women from abuses in the field of abortion and providing them every kind of support in working through the moral issues involved. As Daniel Callahan noted in his discussion with his wife, the important matter is to keep the moral questions in the forefront of this whole consideration of abortion, so that the moral and spiritual issues are honestly faced and every effort is made to create social, medical, and economic conditions so that the need for abortion is reduced to a minimum.[6]

We have avoided any simple determination of the right and the wrong of abortion in this discussion. Our concern has been with the nature of personal and communal life that the discussion reveals. We are, of course, also deeply concerned with the moral and spiritual issues surrounding abortion, and agree heartily that the important question is to keep the moral issues in the forefront of the public debate. Much needs to be said and has been written about the societal structures that generate so much difficulty for women, including impoverishment and unfair employment practices. All of these matters need to be considered in arriving at particular decisions.

There is a further reason for upholding women's right to choose in these and other matters. The deeper issue of personhood arises when one considers choosing and deciding about matters affecting one's life. The churches fought for centuries to uphold women's right to consent in marriage, when patriarchal authority overrode that right. Democratic societies have arisen around the recognition of the centrality of judging and deciding in the unfolding of authentic citizenship. Similarly, judging and deciding are fundamental to the expression of concern in moral actions. Deciding, like loving, is of the very essence of what it means to be a person or to operate as a community. Justice seeks mutuality of life, a mutuality which depends upon the capacities of persons to love and to decide. Laws properly set limits upon the kinds of things that can be decided in a moral community. Unless fetal life is given an absolute value, the burden of proof is upon the society that would remove from women the right to reproductive choice. Until and unless such an absolute value is established (and it is hard to know how this would be done in light of the biological processes we now understand), women's right to choose deserves to be honored.

The deeper problem underlying the abortion controversy is the erosion of any communal context for moral decision making and responsibility. Such moral communities were actually taken for granted in the era of the founders of the Republic, when personal liberty was given such an important place. In this sense, the crisis in public values that comes to the surface in the bitter debate over abortion points to the deeper crisis of the Republic, the erosion of the fabric of communal life. We agree with Daniel Callahan's proposal that the moral issues in abortion should be kept in the forefront of the discussion. However, there is no way that this can happen unless the communal fabric is given its proper place in our common life. This is not simply a matter of interpersonal relations (for institutions govern many aspects of our interpersonal networks), even though those relations are a basic element in any moral and spiritual life.

The reality of power has been the hidden element in this discussion of the debate over abortion; indeed, the struggle between the coalitions in the debate is itself a struggle for the power of women versus power over women. In the case studies, men exercised power over pregnant women in demanding that they seek abortions. The women exercised power over the fetal lives in determining their futures. The stories of the women reveal many experiences of damaging exercise of power over and against them, including rapes and deprivations. In our consideration of love and justice, we have prescinded from the crucial question of power. This was only a provisional step, since power is at the heart of communal relations. We now shift attention to this question of power in the unfolding of concern as love and justice.

Chapter Three

The Moral Web

In *Democracy in America*, Alexis de Tocqueville commented on the importance of freedom and equality in the new Republic. He wondered whether these principles could be held in balance. His insight proved to be prophetic on this issue. When liberty and equality were at odds, as they often were, liberty usually won the day; too often liberty meant freedom in one's own property as well as civil and political liberty. Actually, the Constitutional Convention provided the charter for this path to liberty by refusing to deal with the issue of slavery, leaving the "property" of the slaveholders untouched. As time went on, private property came to mean corporate holdings in land and capital, a far remove from anything in the thoughts of the founders.

The linkage between liberty, which was originally concerned with political freedom, and private property reshaped the meaning of freedom in communal life. Personal liberties were anchored in local communities in the time of the founding. At that time, 95 percent of the population lived in rural areas. The principal settlements were villages and towns; even the cities were small by modern standards. This social reality left its mark on the Constitution, even as the great distances between the states affected thought about representation. The local community was taken as the natural basis for life and liberty, as well as the context for working out problems of inequality. In the late twentieth century, two-thirds of our people dwell in cities, and that percentage increases constantly with the urbanization of suburbia. Urbanization gradually eroded the bonds of local communities. Liberty came to mean freedom to pursue one's own life, independent of neighbors except as one chose to associate. Freedom came to mean autonomy, the pursuit of one's own interests and style of life.

There were and are, to be sure, many constraints on personal autonomy. Marriage and family life preserved communal bonds, yet even marriage has suffered seriously from the erosion of communal bonds. Voluntary associations have labored to support communal life, and, as we noted, the nostalgia for community has reinforced local efforts for community building. In general, however, the ethos of high-tech society engenders isolation of persons and a drive for personal autonomy. This drive, in turn, exacerbates inequalities in wealth and position, lending more and more weight to a kind of possessive individualism.

The strains between personal autonomy and community bonds have created contradictions between the pursuit of freedom and the principle of equality. It is difficult to consider equality when the emphasis of the whole society is upon optimizing one's own interests. This vision of the good life is summarized in a current bumper sticker which reads, "The Man Who Dies with the Most Toys Wins." (It is to be expected that it says "Man.") Lester C. Thurow, the economist, commented on this ethos in an editorial in *The New York Times* of June 14, 1987, observing that business schools are concerned about ethics yet teach that the "sole goal of business managers should be to maximize the net worth of shareholders." The possessive spirit was voiced by Jimmy Bakker who claimed that God wanted his servants to go first class. Freedom becomes distorted to possessiveness in such an ethos, while equality simply goes by the board. In fact, both principles become victims of the real motivation of the high-tech world; this is the enhancement of personal and corporate power as domination and control. Certainly the founders were concerned with power, because they had suffered under the domination of the British crown. They fought for political and civil liberties. They struggled for the freedom to pursue business in their own interests rather than for the coffers of the crown. However, the power they cherished was to be a shared power of a democratic people, not the domination of their communities by corporate wealth. This is the new situation which has created such strains in the Republic, a new situation in which the very meaning as well as organization of power needs to be rethought.

A Communal View of Power

Power plays a crucial role in all of our relationships, from the most personal to the broadest global connections. In religious life, the grasp for absolute dogmas or sacred texts often stems from the desire to gain control over the Mystery, to achieve religious security. The emergence of the national-security states in the late twentieth century is motivated by a similar desire to achieve control. Even possessive individualism is an attempt to gain control over one's life and obligations.

The future is always uncertain in our human world. The responses of other persons are equally uncertain. Human life is shot through with uncertainty. One response to such uncertainties is to struggle for control, especially when communal bonds have eroded and expectations have become unclear. Under these conditions, power becomes domination or struggle for control over life. Achieving a reasonable level of control is, of course, a perfectly sensible course of action; however, the Western world moved more and more toward an illusory kind of control that violated personal and communal liberties as well as reasonable expectations. As communal bonds eroded, life became more and more uncertain, and the drive for control became obsessive.

Public communalism is also prone to employ power as control, leading to excesses and violation of liberties. There is a long history of tyranny of communal powers over persons. Even as we explore the possibilities of public communalism, we do well to keep that human record in mind. As communal beings, we identify with our important communities, seeking security through our membership. We often become dependent upon those communities, even as we seek autonomy in pursuit of our interests. This is a strange paradox of personal life, the drive to autonomy that in turn leads to isolation and unthinking identification with a people or nation. Individualism has this dual character, drawing persons toward isolated pursuits and leaving them prone to fanatical nationalism or religious bigotry. The erosion of communal life creates a vacuum of power that is all too readily filled by military adventurism and nationalistic rhetoric. These are perversions of power that point us to the question of the true nature of power in human life.

Reflecting on the meaning of power is reminiscent of Augustine's observation that we know what time is until we begin to think about it. We think and talk about power in our ordinary routines. We speak of money as power, implying that it gives control. We speak of a powerful team or a power hitter, meaning the capacity to win. We speak of some politicians as power seekers, implying that they want to gain control rather than serve the voters. Thus, power as power over things or others is familiar in our everyday discourse. In this sense, power does seem to be domination or control for us. There is good reason for this conventional view. In the early days of Western science, Francis Bacon spoke of the promise of science as giving us power over nature. Thomas Hobbes and Niccolò Machiavelli did much to imprint the idea of power as domination on Western politics. The emergence of capitalism opened the door to competition to gain power over resources and markets.

The idea of domination is a unilateral view of power. In this perspective, power flows in one direction: from those who are, for whatever reason, stronger, down upon those who are forced to submit to their control. In this kind of a struggle for power, there are winners and losers, those who gain control and those who lose control. It pictures the world as a zero-sum game, in which the winners can gain only when others lose.

This understanding of power as domination is so deeply ingrained in our lives that it seems quixotic to challenge it. Nevertheless, the inward bondedness of personal being implies that we have missed the real nature and meaning of power, for communal beings are not ultimately caught up in a zero-sum game. A zero-sum game is the playing field of isolated individuals. If we return to our discussion of the social context of personal development, we find a very different experience of power, far removed from the zero-sum game. Parents, of course, have a dominant position over their children, by virtue of age, size, experience, and control of resources. However, a wise parent knows that bringing children to maturity comes about through nurture, give and take, listening as well as telling, learning from one another as well as teaching. Power in socialization is mutual, moving in two directions, unless it has become oppressive and crippling. Influence upon children (or in any relationship) derives from mutual exchange, respect, and trust. Obedience can be elicited temporarily through force or domination, but it disappears as soon as the threat of force is gone. Real influence is internal to relationships, built upon the inward bonding of persons in communal life or the mutual organizational supports of corporate life. True influence depends upon mutual bonds. This is also a clue to the real nature of power.

A relational understanding of personal and communal life reveals that *power is the exercise of life in mutuality*; life is a multi-lateral play of human capacities, an interchange of powers and concerns that enriches human possibilities. We touch here upon the fundamental nature of power. We do not create power, nor do we possess power in this authentic sense. We dwell in and through the communal energies that flow in life, binding us to nature, to one another and to our world. We share in these energies, exercising them as capacities and skills through loving, working, and deciding. We are inwardly bonded with one another and with nature through the interplay of the powers of life.

What, then, does it mean for a person to exercise power in this fundamental sense? What does it mean to speak of power as the "exercise of life?"

On a personal level, exercise of life is the capacity to love, to work, and to decide. Love is often contrasted with power, since love may mean sacrificing, while power is taken to mean winning or dominating. However, love unfolds power in the true sense, for loving is the capacity to give as well as receive, to sustain relationships amid the tensions of conflicting needs and interests. Loving is the true power of personal life, for it can bear opposition without surrendering personal integrity or breaking relationships. This is the real meaning of dialogue, the continued unfolding of differences and common possibilities in communities and organizations. The exercise of life is, thus, the unfolding of the bonds of communal and organizational life, the exercise of love in mutuality.

The exercise of life is also the capacity to work, the power to make and create, to alter our world in ways that meet our needs and aspirations. Work is our power to maintain our lives, to reproduce the human species, to care for the next generation in home, school, and neighborhood. These are not powers that we own or possess. They are ways in which we share in the flow of power that is sustaining all of life in the cosmos. We share these powers in trust for the sake of personal and global life. So it is with the food we grow, the clothing we manufacture, the metals we forge, the technical instruments we devise, the scientific knowledge we generate, and the arts we cultivate. These are capacities and skills, energies and resources, that we humans share as a species on this small planet. Working, in this basic sense, is the sustaining and unfolding of our mutual bondedness with earth and one another. It is the exercise of life in which love finds concrete expression, nurturing the young, cleaning a house, cooking a meal, tilling a field, developing a vaccine in a laboratory, creating a work of art. Working unfolds our community with one another as the exercise of power in mutuality.

Deciding is another aspect of the exercise of life in mutuality, the expression of power in community. We do not usually think of deciding as so central to the exercise of life, yet judging, choosing, and deciding unfold power in communal life. On the most personal side, our decisions in love and work determine our future and the relationships for which we are responsible. Our judgments as to right and wrong, good and bad, are political aspects of our personal life, ways in which we exercise power for mutuality or domination. The same holds for decisions about our ultimate commitments, things for which we are willing to make sacrifices or even give our lives. Like loving and working, deciding unfolds our collaboration with others, with our natural environment, and with our world.

If essential power is the exercise of life in mutuality, how is it possible that power as domination could gain such prominence in Western life? Is there not an authentic place for control in life? Certainly control has been a basic value in the technical development of the human species. Moreover, the search for security within reasonable limits is an inclination that is shared by all peoples. It would seem that the unilateral exercise of power is a possibility intrinsic to the mutuality of power. We can appreciate this if we turn to the metaphoric character of all relationships. In the mutuality of personal relations, we know ourselves as similar to others and yet different from them. If the other person were utterly alien or different, we could experience "it" only as irrelevant or simply nonexistent for us. On the other hand, if we experience another person as similar to us up to the point of pure identity, we have lost all sense of our own unique being. We are familiar with both of these extremes in relation to other persons. The sense of utter difference or dissimilarity characterizes relationships in which other persons are despised or excluded from our group. Racial, class, ethnic, religious, and other alienations reflect this radicalization of difference. The metaphoric interpretation, then, takes the form of a stereotype of the other person. The other side of the coin is the identification of a parent with a child, a man with his wife, or a woman with her husband. Such total identification is utter dependency, even a kind of addiction, in which the real integrity of self and other dissolves to the detriment of both.

Mutuality in the exercise of life sustains the tension between similarity and difference, binding us to others in the similarity of belonging, yet setting us apart from one another as ourselves. In this sense, ego identity emerges as a metaphoric disclosure through our bonding and distance from one another. Our capacity for increasing the distance between ourselves and others or things enables us to see more objectively. Such distance is not only useful in technical efforts but preserves us from demands that are intrusive or inappropriate. We exist in mutual bonds with nature, dependent yet independent. Our capacity for distancing ourselves enables us to gain predictability and control in many of our exchanges with nature and even in certain interpersonal situations, such as business negotiations. Such "controlling" relationships are constructive so long as they do not become unilateral exercises of power over things or others. When we obscure the mutuality of life, we begin to damage the natural world and violate the communal bonds of personal life. The same holds true in the exercise of the powers of life in education, economic life, and political action. Our capacity for distance, for being for ourselves, lends a measure of control that establishes reliable expectations. The exaggeration of distance to the point of breaking mutuality creates an alienated natural and/or social environment.

Our capacity for distance presupposes our collaboration with nature and others. If we did not belong to this world, we would live only in lonely isolation. Thus, the excesses of distance distort the bonds of mutuality, creating pathological relationships within our natural and human environments. Instead of a creative metaphor of mutuality of life, alienated power lives by a metaphor of domination over life, taking the forms of manipulation or seduction or violent suppression.

These perversions of power relations are violations of the communal being of persons and peoples. However, if the bonding of life in mutuality is our essential way of being as human, how is it possible that power in history has been so grossly distorted? Why should the human species break the mutuality of life, when its powers and virtues arise within the bonds of natural and personal relationships? Whence the search for security that generates such drives for domination? These are the difficult questions that may give us clues to the crisis of values in the Western world and in the Republic. Possessive values seem to have triumphed, yet communal values are paramount in the movements which we have traced.

Roots of Alienation and Domination

Security has become a major concern in Western societies. In one respect, this is not unusual, since life is insecure at the best. We are constantly being reminded of the extinction of animal and botanical species in our time. We are also conscious of the threat to all of life on earth that is posed by nuclear weaponry. On a personal level, we experience the impact of diseases that threaten life; some, like AIDS, reach epidemic proportions. Moreover, our economic system threatens us with changes that may mean poverty and unemployment for millions of people. Human life has always been prey to natural forces that could spell disaster, but now the economic system that was to give control has itself become a source of insecurity.

Although we have no way of knowing what threats to life may mean to other species, we do know that human beings are conscious of threats to their well-being because they anticipate future possibilities. Human beings live with a sense of the future that intensifies their feelings of uncertainty. We are linguistic and imaginative enough to project scenarios that can increase our fears for the future. We traced this process earlier in the scenarios that were projected by the case of a woman considering abortion. Our capacity for creating scenarios can enrich our lives, but it also opens up a world of unforeseeable dangers. The search for a reasonable level of security, in this context, would be willingness to live with the tension of promises and threats without undue fear. This would mean achieving a sense of security that can cope with ordinary contingencies. In fact, cultures and peoples have their own codes for determining appropriate risks and threats. This includes the degree of risk that is considered appropriate for particular tasks. Study of the Trobriand Islanders, for example, revealed that they took considerable risks on their trading journeys at sea in what was called the Kula. This dangerous voyage was hedged about with special rituals for the building and preparation of the vessels that would hazard the journey. In societies like our own that put a high premium on change and innovation, there are many uncertainties about the future; in fact, our whole way of life creates a rather high level of anxiety and insecurity. Traditionalism gave some protection to many peoples under these conditions, but our own society has eschewed tradition for innovation and suffers a corresponding anxiety about the future. The development of nuclear weaponry is a dramatic case in point. Insecurities generate strong impulses to gain power over whatever forces may be threatening disaster. There is, thus, a vicious circle within high-tech society, whereby rapid changes and insecurity lead in turn to further attempts at technical control and innovation. In these circumstances, there are powerful motivations for seeking power over any conditions, persons, or groups that may challenge our enterprises.

Nevertheless, anxiety about future threats does not seem to provide an adequate account of the human predilection for seeking power over others. We can appreciate this when we consider how much the drive for domination leads to violence. Violence may well be as old as human society; however, the Western world has experienced a level of violence that is probably unmatched in human history. Economic exploitation and violent suppression of protest in the twentieth century have certainly raised serious questions about the communal character of the human species. The experience of two world wars, the Holocaust, and the nightmare of aggression in Southeast Asia raise fundamental questions about the roots of domination in the human species. How can one account for such insatiable impulses to dominate?

If we build upon the understanding of insecurity and anxiety about the future, we may trace the roots of domination to our linguistic and metaphoric way of being as humans. In our naming of our world, we take a kind of possession of things, a kind of mastery over them. This is an unconscious but nonetheless real process. We assume that we know what this or that is. Moreover, that process of identifying things is loaded with values, for our naming includes a way in which the thing is to be viewed or treated, what its possible use may be, and what, if any, threat it may pose. Much of our early education teaches children that certain things, such as sharp knives or busy streets, are dangerous. We are in possession of a useable world through the language that we learn. This is the world that we take for granted, as sociologist Alfred Schutz was wont to put it. It is our predictable world, and, within limits, it is relatively certain.

We have noted the metaphoric character of language and our unfolding of the world through metaphoric transformations. We discussed the metaphoric character of the scenarios projected by women deciding about abortion. We also touched upon the metaphoric interplay of love and justice in moral decisions. However, we have not considered the ambiguity of a world that is metaphoric and, thus, open to question. Metaphors, as we noted, involve a play of similarity and difference; consequently, that which comes to language in metaphor is always open to reinterpretation. This is especially true on a personal level. We think we know someone very well and, thus, know what to expect in the relationship. Then, much to our astonishment, the person acts in a way that we would never have anticipated. Strangely enough, our knowledge of the everyday world is just as uncertain. For practical purposes, the things that we use are what they are, while in another sense they are whirling flows of energy in particular shapes. We manage rather well with this world that has come into language, so long as we do not think about it too much. Then, the tension of similarity and difference comes to the surface, and the unanticipated is at the doorstep.

Metaphoric disclosures come about through a conflict of meanings, yet a conflict in which one meaning wins out without obliterating the other meaning. For example, Jesus interpreted God as father in his teachings. He taught the disciples to use the name Father for God in prayer. In this metaphoric disclosure about God, Jesus drew upon an earlier tradition that was not very familiar. He brought the term *father* into conjunction with the Sacred Mystery, God. There is a flow of meaning between the two terms that is revealing about both symbols. God is understood in parental terms, and God's parenthood is explicated in the parable of the prodigal son; that is, God is interpreted as a loving, forgiving father rather than a harsh, judgmental parent. In turn, the term *father* is being modified, for parenting is given a sacred connotation of loving and caring. In this instance, however, the important transformation is the illumination of an aspect of the Mystery, a quality of love and forgiveness. God is now understood differently, for a reinterpreted parental image has given new meaning to the Mighty Ruler, Judge, and Lord. From that time on, followers of Jesus were able to open their prayers with the expression, Our Father.

Another aspect of metaphor is immediately apparent with this example. Metaphors transform accepted meanings, disclosing new understandings, but they do so by creating a tension between the similar and the different. Jesus teaches that God is like a father in certain respects. He also teaches about judgments and powers in God's reign that no father or parent possesses. God is at once father and different from any father. The creative, revelatory quality in the metaphoric teaching flows from the tension within the sentence, God is our father; the very unexpected juxtaposition impressed Jesus' followers and they preserved it in their testimony and liturgy. A metaphor brings dissimilar realities into similarity, creating new insight. This happens constantly in the natural sciences, where astrophysicists talk about "big bangs" and "black holes." As expressions are used again and again, they are taken for granted and become ordinary expressions, or what we call "literal meanings" (which are, in fact, accepted metaphoric expressions). In this case, the tension of similarity and difference erodes, and we simply speak of things as this or that.

There is a reason why certain metaphors are accepted as clear or certain knowledge of this or that. There is within the metaphoric disclosure, for example, "God is Father," an implied identity of the terms *God* and *Father*. It is a tensive identity, in the sense that important metaphors always retain the strains between similarity and difference. However, God is addressed simply as Father in the Lord's Prayer. The worshiper does not say, God, Who is like a Father. He or she says, Our Father. In this sense, the metaphor always implies an identity that has come about through the metaphoric transformation. One can address God simply as Father, even though the tension remains within the metaphoric disclosure. This is the persuasive power of a generative or creative metaphor. It creates a new image of reality.

When a metaphoric event such as Jesus' teaching about God's fatherhood becomes generative, creating a whole new understanding that influences a community, it becomes a permanent symbol. Symbols arise from such important metaphoric events, disclosures that are persuasive and generative within a community. Symbols like the emancipation of the Exodus arise through events in which decisive meanings are disclosed to a people. The flight from Egypt is interpreted through the metaphor of a going out under the guidance of Yahweh. The freeing of the slaves in the midst of the Civil War gains a permanent place in the Republic through the title Emancipation Proclamation. Such symbols retain the tension that is present within the original metaphoric event.

The fatherhood of God became an accepted symbol in the Christian tradition, and, as usually happens with important symbols, the tension was concealed and God was taken to be Our Father. This imagery fit very well into the patriarchal cultures of the Hellenistic and Roman worlds, so that God's fatherhood undergirded paternal authority, while patriarchy lent its own meaning to God's fatherhood. Symbols drift with history in this way, undergoing modification and reinterpretation with changing social and political realities. However, the tensive metaphoric root of the symbol is always there, creating the possibility of a critique of the symbol by reopening awareness of the difference that is buried within it. This is precisely what has happened in the struggle of feminist theology against patriarchy. Feminist critique reopened the metaphoric difference within the symbolism of God's fatherhood, making it possible to use other terms for speaking of the Mystery, including the image of God's motherhood. Thus, feminist critique restored the tensive quality of the identity that is implied in the metaphor, God is Our Father, recovering the difference which had been hidden by customary usage.

The identity implied in the metaphor God is Father bears within it a hidden tension between *is* and *is not*: God *is* Father, yet God *is not* Father. The identity that is implied in a metaphoric symbol reveals the being of what is. When an astrophysicist speaks of a "black hole," he or she is making an effort to say what this phenomenon is. Other scientists who challenge this interpretation will very likely use other metaphors to symbolize what is being described. The critique of a symbol, religious or other, reopens the tension between *is* and *is not*. Whether it be the symbol of "manifest destiny" or "fatherland" or any other symbol, the possibility of critique is always present, especially when the symbol has become oppressive or destructive or deceptive.

In everyday life, the ambiguity of *is* and *is not* makes little or no difference. In our taken-for-granted world, we simply assume that things are what they are and use them or enjoy them as such. However, the *is not* is there, constantly undermining our surface security in our world. The earth is not the solid terra firma on which we can be secure, though for most purposes it can simply be treated as such. If an earthquake strikes, we become aware that the earth is a moving inferno which can destroy everything we cherish. On an everyday level, we experience this uncertainty when a close friend gives a radically different interpretation of something that we took for granted and that we believed both of us saw in the same way. Our fixed world is never more than a world about which we have concealed our doubts and uncertainties—and well we might, for no one can live long in a state of constant doubt about the world. We let the *is not* slip into obscurity, but it is always there, appearing at the most unlikely moments. This is strikingly true of the *is not* of our own being, which we take for granted until something brings to mind the reality that we are also bearers of death, of our own *is not*.

The *is not* is also creative when it intrudes upon our lives. The encounter with the unexpected, the new reality, makes new experience possible. The unanticipated sets the stage for learning. Thomas Edison, for example, never took for granted that things had to be simply the way they were, at least in fields of his particular interest. Similarly, the sciences develop from questions and troubling facts that do not fit accepted theories. It is the new, different, even threatening possibilities that awaken us to new understanding. The *is not* challenges us as well as creating uncertainty in our taken-for-granted world. Even the awareness of our mortality often brings us to our senses when we are wasting our gifts or even our lives. The metaphoric character of our linguistic world creates both uncertainty and challenge, insecurity and capacity for creativity. When the *is not* can be borne with trust (or with what religious people call *faith*) in life and relationships, then change and challenge can be creative. Yet, most societies and people, even those of faith, fear the insecurity of the *is not*. They suppress their fears, and often try to push the uncertainties away by striving to control their situations and those around them. Instead of thriving on the mutuality of life in sharing and loving, they attempt to master uncertainty, establishing institutions that dominate and control people and the natural world. This refusal of the uncertainty of our world leads to enmity with nature and alienation from other people. Our passion to control the natural and human worlds paves the way for violence.

Our struggles to overcome the uncertainties of life through domination create deeper anxieties, for our control is never complete, even though it may seem so on the surface. This is especially true of the institutions that give a permanent structure to domination, since they are not so accessible to challenge as interpersonal relations. Institutions need not create structures of compulsion and domination, though they tend to do so in order to preserve their power. Business enterprises are normally dedicated to innovation for the sake of growth, yet they often repeat successful patterns in order to avoid risk. This happened to Detroit's auto industry at the very height of its success in the 1950s and 1960s. Suddenly the pattern of success was overturned by small foreign cars, and the industry is still struggling to regain its place in the market. The same kind of thing happens with schools, religious communities, families, neighborhoods, cities, and nations.

Many institutions corrupt their leaders by investing them with a false sense of power. They insulate the leadership from the uncertainties that threaten them. Before they know it, the *is not* has thrown all of their calculations into chaos. Stalin's paranoid drive to control Soviet Russia blinded him to the real threat of the German invasion, almost leading to the annihilation of the country. In his insatiable drive for power, Hitler led his country into a disastrous war and brought the horrors of the Holocaust onto the Jewish people. In both cases, institutions established distance so that those who perpetrated the monstrous deeds assumed they were serving their countries. They suppressed the signs of uncertainty that surrounded them, stamping them out when they surfaced. Time and again Hitler's generals came to the Wolf's Lair to convince him that they were losing the war, only to leave with the conviction that Germany was invincible. The attempt by the South African government to suppress black aspirations for freedom is one of the most bitter examples in the latter part of the twentieth century of this kind of paranoid pursuit of power. The United States likewise has a long history of segregating black people and cultivating paranoid illusions about dangers they pose to their neighborhoods and workplaces.

Our insecurities and our capacity to remove ourselves from the realities around us combine to freeze us within rigid systems of domination. Failures and challenges from others, especially from those who are oppressed by our systems, may break through this distance and awaken us to realities. Then, we can learn and find ways to move toward mutuality and shared power. However, the fear of the *is not* that pervades all of life leads all too often to dominating parents, organized racism, and exploitation of poor people. The passion for security leads too often to possessive institutions and even possessive societies. Then, the cry of the poor and oppressed is not heard or is silenced by violence. The tragedy of this passion for security in an insecure world is that it undermines the very certainties that it imagines can be won by domination. Possessiveness is its own undoing in a world that is grounded in shared, communal being.

The confessional traditions of the West—Jewish, Muslim, and Christian—treat this human passion for total security as rebellion against the Divine Mystery. The Christian tradition refers to this rebellion as sin. If we recognize that humans dwell in an uncertain world, between *is* and *is not*, we can acknowledge the importance of what has been called sin in these traditions. Sin, in this sense, is the expropriation of the shared powers of human mutuality by persons, institutions, and nations. Since, according to these traditions, the shared power of life flows from the Divine Mystery through all of creation, violation of the power of the neighbor is rebellion against God. Exploitation of the weak by the strong, the poor by the rich, and the oppressed by the oppressors violates the fundamental mutuality that constitutes human beings and their communities. Such exploitation is usually embedded in institutions that are thought to be neutral, whereas, in fact, they are systems of compulsion that violate the very foundations of human existence. Whether defined in confessional terms or through insight into the nature of human existence, the inclination to domination is always present and can only be offset by institutions that fulfill human claims to mutuality of life.

The Western world fell into the error of establishing the struggle for power over nature and people as its basic way of life. Instead of building economic institutions that preserved mutuality of life, the West gave legitimacy to domination in economic life. This was done in the name of a free market, but no market is free when some have more power and money than others, and especially when some gain an excess of power through the labor of others. The West, however, also moved toward liberal democratic politics in order to preserve the market from control by the state. This political process has provided leverage for protest against economic structures of compulsion. Corporate economic powers have all too often dominated democratic politics as well, but there is always room in the liberal heritage to challenge this economic domination. Thus, the possessive society was institutionalized in the West, while the countervailing force of liberal politics was also established. What Max Weber referred to as the "iron cage" of bureaucratic domination is not, then, a total cage, for there are avenues of access to its system of constraint.

The basic mutuality of human life means that people are never willing to be dominated, however long they may have to wait in order to rebel. Democratic politics is a basic institution through which such rebellion can be implemented. Moreover, the uncertainties of reality and of our linguistic world mean that no institution is eternal, not even the church. We dwell between the *is* and *is not*. We cannot secure our world against the new, the challenging, and the threatening, no matter how carefully we try. Our hope is that we can learn to live with reasonable levels of uncertainty, to share with one another, and to establish boundaries that protect us from our own and others' inclination to dominate. Distortions of power in personal and institutional life will not disappear with a wave of the democratic flag; however, there are resources in the constitution of human communities for preserving justice and a proper exercise of power in mutuality. The metaphoric process that creates a communal world, however uncertain, also furnishes us with moral grounds for preserving a communal world.

The Texture of Moral Experience

We are unfinished beings, constantly changing, gaining new insights about ourselves and discovering things about our pasts that we had forgotten or tried to forget. Human life is a process of discovery, some of it painful, some enjoyable. It is not very pleasant to learn from others that we are being grumpy or nasty. It is gratifying to hear that we have been helpful. These interpersonal exchanges shape who we are and fashion whatever communities we share.

Language or discourse is only one aspect of these interpersonal networks. There are times of silence, times of shared enjoyment of music or theater. Yet, our discourse is the clearest expression of ourselves to one another, revealing who we are and building a common life. Our linguistic experience gives us the most important insights into the essential elements of personal relationships. We come to be as persons in the network of communication.

We have examined the threefold pattern of metaphoric disclosure in discourse, the conjoining of the different in uncovering a similarity that yields a tensive identity. The wife who comments that "her husband is an old bear" may be setting the stage for others to remark, upon seeing him approach, "here comes the old bear." Metaphors that are apt usually stick, as is often the case with nicknames. As we noted above, metaphors usually fade into taken-for-granted meanings, becoming part of the ordinary vocabulary of daily discourse. The metaphoric interplay of similarity, difference, and tensive identity is the creative mode of disclosure in discourse. It is the process by which meaning originates. As the mode of disclosure of meaning, metaphoric process is also the way in which personal being is disclosed in interpersonal life. We come to be as persons through a process of communication in which metaphor is central. To this extent, the threefold character of metaphor provides important clues to the texture of moral experience, revealing the way in which persons are bound to one another in moral communities of responsibility, yet liberated as independent beings.

So far as we know, all peoples have developed moral codes to shape their common life. So long as there are people dwelling in community, there are moral codes to order their conduct. We humans do not live by instinct but by the symbols that give pattern to our world. However much moral symbols may change over time, they seem to have similar patterns. Hence, the metaphoric disclosure of personal bonds and moral claims reflects the imperatives of the Western heritage, yet also points to common or universal elements in all human relationships. Since the metaphoric process is integral to all human linguistic experience, there may be enormous variety of symbolizations but there will also be common patterns of human bonding. Other cultures and traditions symbolize these bonds in accord with their experiences and histories, but ultimately they all deal with the moral claims of persons and communities.

Three elements of justice emerged in the West as basic symbols of the moral life: freedom, equality, and community. It is evident that in all serious decisions freedom or responsibility to decide and awareness of the claims of equality are major elements (community will be considered below). This play of freedom and equality seems to originate in our earliest experiences, leading to personal and moral development. The basic rhythms of personal relations seem to express this play of freedom and equality, for the give and take of conversations preserves a tensive duality of contributing and receiving, speaking and listening. When these basic rhythms are broken, communal bonds are strained. When conversations become one-sided, they cease to be shared experiences and become boring monologues. The metaphoric process reflects these rhythms that weave the moral web, bringing to discourse the play of life, making possible a common world. These elements of justice are not, then, an imposition of moral order by society on amoral persons. They are not simply conventions created to control behavior. Human creativity and innovation do enter into the symbolizing and ordering of justice, but they do not create such an order out of whole cloth. Freedom, equality, and community are integral elements in all interpersonal experience. Particular societies may and do symbolize these elements differently; moreover, one culture may give more weight to freedom than to equality, or to community than to either freedom or equality. However, so long as discourse is of the essence of human life, the human being as a deciding center within a community of persons deserving equal respect and voice will constitute the basic structure of a moral order.

The decisions about abortion that we considered earlier also revealed the ways in which different resolutions of the tension of freedom and equality can be adjudicated. When the decision favored the abortion, the freedom of women to have a future took precedence over the claim of the fetal life to equal respect and consideration. When the decision favored carrying the fetus to term, the claim of equal respect and consideration took precedence over the freedom of the mother to find an adequate future. In this sense, freedom is bound up with equality, for one or the other claim to equal freedom had to be sacrificed. Since the pregnant woman carried the power of decision for both herself and the fetus, she had to determine the weight which would be given to their different futures. We can see in this process how the implicit sense of identity arises in the play of difference and similarity. In the case of fetal life, the sense of identity arising from the experience of similarity and difference can be deceptive, since the fetus is not yet a person (this is the case in at least some views of fetal life). If the identity is taken as absolute, concealing the tension within the experience, then there can be no possibility of an abortion. This is the moral path taken by those who argue for an absolute right to birth. In getting an abortion in order to make possible a workable future, a woman would be sacrificing another person for her own future. However, if the difference between the mother and the fetal life is maintained as a significant difference in personal being, then the right to choice remains and the difficult decision falls to the woman as to which course to follow.

We can translate this moral network to the level of persons in community. Community arises through our inward bonding as personal beings, as we have observed. We come to be as persons through our communal bonds. We do not come to be as persons and then negotiate a set of personal connections. In this sense, equality in respect and power are prior in our personal being, for the bonding through which we mature is the generative process in personal life. However, the metaphoric tension in this process means that freedom of persons is always essential to the realization of equality in community. The centering of life in personhood is an essential element in any possible community. In fact, a community is a network of persons sharing common symbols and values; by the same token, the person is the community seen from a particular, indispensable perspective.

We noted earlier how communities have sometimes suppressed personal freedom, defining equality as a sameness under communal authority. This is another way of understanding the imposition of the right to birth on women and the suppression of their right to choice. Communities can become moral dictators, especially when they feel uncertain about their moral order. The metaphoric process suggests that the moral texture of interpersonal life is better understood as a tension between personal freedom and equality within the embrace of a shared, common life. Our Western experience has tended to play down the importance of common life and values, entrusting the well-being of the community to the play of freedom in the market and the preservation of equal rights in contracts. Since both freedom and equal rights are shaped by the character of the common life, the lack of common values has given free play to struggles for power and advantage. Equal right has too often come to mean the right to exploit private property to the disadvantage of the poor and of the community. The problem of the West, and thus of the world that is so dominated by the West, is to achieve a modicum of consensus on common values, so that freedom and equality can be creative rather than destructive elements in our world.

In recognizing the prior reality of community or similarity in the texture of moral life, we also encounter the tendency of communities to become closed and exclusive. The inclination to closure is only another expression of the attempt to overcome insecurity in an uncertain world. When we can create a sense of sameness with our own family or group or neighborhood or nation, we can achieve a spurious sense that we are safe in this world. Such exclusive symbols of identity play up separateness and difference over against other peoples, as though one's own community were the only true expression of similarity. We are alike and all others are unlike. Ours is the true community. The others are aliens or "an evil empire" or heretics or simply enemies. Individuals also display this kind of exclusiveness in what we call egoism or a kind of egocentric life. In the extreme form, we speak of this as narcissism, the determination of all meanings in terms of one's own desires, fears, and interests. These are pathologies of personal life, just as absolutizing one's community is a pathology of communal life.

Despite these pathological tendencies in personal and communal life, there remains nonetheless an openness in the metaphoric process that subverts such exclusiveness. Karsten Harries noted this openness of the metaphoric process in his discussion of poetry.[1] He views a poem as an extended metaphor, creating a mood and revealing an aspect of our world. He also notes that a poem strives for a wholeness or completeness in itself, bringing us to rest in its quiet disclosure. A metaphor, however, bears within itself the tension of difference, so that the quiet sense of wholeness created by a poem always opens out upon a transcendence of which it is only a hint. In other terms, a poem points beyond itself to possibilities that it never fully captures, for it bears within itself what we have called the *is not*.

Along these lines we have argued that story or extended metaphor is the best expression of our being as persons and communities. Our stories are never ended, though they are always ending. Our stories, like our lives, bear their *is not* within them. They point beyond themselves to possibilities that may generate hope or despair, to possibilities of meaning which we have designated the religious dimension of existence. The metaphoric quality of the narrative preserves the sense of completeness in our story without bringing it to closure or a false sense of absoluteness. Thus, we live with our stories in an open world, ever meeting new possibilities. In a similar way, our communities have a metaphoric thrust toward other communities, toward universal community. Guilt assails those communities that denigrate others; at least one finds that they spend a great deal of time justifying their stereotypes or discriminatory practices. The metaphoric character of justice points toward a larger human community than the closed fellowships in which we pass so much of our lives. We are meant to be citizens of the world, for we dwell in similarity and equality with all peoples, even as we rightly claim the freedom to preserve our own communities of responsibility.

The consideration of open and closed communities brings into play the tension between justice and power. Our closed communities are usually attempts to preserve our power and security over against others. On the other hand, the essential openness of communities as metaphoric events points to the shared reality of power, for our security is actually maintained through our common life and mutuality. We have argued that power is the exercise of life in the mutuality of personal being. We also noted that power can be and often is expropriated from this shared life for private or corporate advantage. The preempting of the power of others is a sundering of the bonds between similarity and difference, since it elevates difference to an absolute claim. The individual or corporate body takes upon itself the right to hold power over others, elevating its particularity to an absolute claim to domination. This is the injustice of domination. It breaks the interplay of freedom and equality within community. Domination in its various forms is a violation of the mutuality of life. Sexism, racism, class oppression, and imperialism are gross expressions of this denial of mutuality. On a practical level, this manifests itself as dumping homeless women and children into hotel rooms, excluding minority peoples from decent jobs, or sending proxy armies of mercenaries to bleed peasant communities that refuse to bow down to the "great power." Each of these instances of domination reflects an institutional expression of domination that reaches far beyond the scale of interpersonal rivalries and antagonisms.

When we speak of community we usually think only along personal lines. However, community is sustained by the institutional systems that embody its symbols and values, its rules and sanctions. The family is, perhaps, the only major institution that operates on an intimately interpersonal level. Most of our institutions are on a larger, less personal scale, such as factories, universities, government agencies, and international organizations. It is within this institutional network that we shall have to explore the working out of the problems of power and justice.

The expropriation of power is endemic to human societies, since life "between *is* and *is not*" is always to a degree uncertain and insecure. Some institutions can reduce these anxieties. Others seem designed to increase insecurity. We shall have to explore these institutional questions later. For the moment, it is important to recognize that struggles for power make conflict endemic to human life. Conflict, however, is not always violent. It may simply mean confrontations in which the claims to freedom and equal respect are defended against impositions and domination. Struggles for justice on personal and institutional levels are, thus, part and parcel of a healthy, democratic life. Where such struggles are suppressed, the exercise of life in mutuality is violated and injustice is imposed by force.

Struggles for justice set up profound tensions between love and justice. We noted above that love is very close to justice, as evidenced in our anger at injustices suffered by those we love. However, love strives to maintain the mutuality of life amid conflict, while justice presses for the claims of those whose right to respect and voice have been violated. Love never surrenders concern for mutuality, even amid the most agonizing struggles for justice. In this sense, love and justice express the two sides of the mutuality of life—the bonding of life and respect for the particularity of persons and communities. This is where the power of love to forgive can overcome alienation, even amid our struggles for justice, without subverting the legitimate claims of the parties involved. Mandela, Biko, and Tutu in South Africa have manifested this capacity to hold love and justice together in the struggle of black people against the violence of their government. Martin Luther King, Jr., was able to lead the civil rights struggle in the United States to victory through his remarkable capacity to fight for justice in the spirit of love. Communal life survives only where love and justice are joined to sustain mutuality of life in full recognition of the freedom and equality of persons. Thus, love, power, and justice enter as equal partners in the weaving of the moral web.

Communal life is organized, as we indicated above, in patterns of institutional life such as schools, workplaces, and homes. This institutional order embodies degrees of justice and injustice. Some, like institutional racism in the United States or apartheid in South Africa, are simply orders of violence and injustice. Others, like many schools today, are a mix of justice and injustice, making an advantage look like an achievement for the privileged, as Ivan Illich puts it, while still offering some opportunity for the less privileged. Institutions organize how status is defined, how rewards are distributed, how power is allocated, and how one kind of good rather than another is produced. In a high-tech society like ours, these institutional networks are extremely complex and far reaching in their impact. As we explore public communalism, we shall have to investigate the ways in which justice and injustice become embodied in our institutions.

Chapter Four
The Organization of Work

Work is a primary, if not the foremost, activity of the human species. The priority of work may be most characteristic of the West, yet the survival of peoples has always depended upon their work. This is not to discount the many other activities, from recreation to aesthetic enjoyment and celebration, that make life worth living. Yet, it is work that keeps the lifeblood flowing in a society. This is true, at least, if one understands by work the many ways in which human beings cope with their day-to-day existence. This means everything from nursing a child to building a house to conducting an experiment to suffering through an illness. In this most general sense, we are all workers.

Some work is conducted in a spontaneous fashion, but most of a people's work is organized in institutions. Child care is carried on in families, day-care centers, nurseries, and schools. Learning is organized in classes and schools. Public services are organized through villages, towns, and municipalities. These institutional structures provide the networks of guidance, support, and standards by which work is sustained. Continuous production and distribution, whether in providing meals in a home or manufacturing refrigerators, require regular patterns of activity and expectations.

73

Institutions bear much of the power in human societies. When one reflects on the justice or injustice of certain conditions of life, it is finally the institution that comes under scrutiny. Is there favoritism in the classroom? Has the public official conducted himself or herself in a dishonest or unethical manner without reprimand from the government? It is the organization of human activity that bears the power and weight of society's continuing life. So far as work is concerned, institutions are organized to maintain production and manage a reasonable kind of distribution of rewards and services. This network of institutions is usually called the economy.

Discussion of the economy has been so wrapped in mystification by the economists, that most citizens either throw up their hands or ignore the issues completely. However, economics has always come down to who works, what kind of work is done, and how work is organized. In the classical period, economy simply meant management of the household or, in our terms, the organization of productive and reproductive work in household life. Since much of that society was organized as a slave system, women and slaves carried on both kinds of work or labor. Despite the pretensions of economics to be a "natural" science of the laws of production and distribution, any economy is at its base an organization of reproductive and productive work. This is not to deny the complexity that is introduced into the economy with the global distribution of commodities, the centrality of capital, and the global market in resources, goods, and money. However, if we stick to the basic meaning of economy as the organization of work, we shall continue with the concrete perspective of our inquiry into the inward bonds of persons and communities. Whatever complexity is required to enrich this basic structure can be introduced as seems appropriate. Nevertheless, too much mystification surrounds the rather obvious difficulties that now plague our reproductive and productive life. We need not allow "supply side" or "monetary" or other kinds of rhetoric to confuse the issues. We are confronting some very elemental issues about the organization of human work in our society and our world. It is important that all citizens feel free to reflect on their lives and the work that they do.

The Crisis of Productive and Reproductive Work

The core of the present economic crisis has been formulated by Madonna Kolbenschlag in an essay titled, "The Politics of Inequality and the Challenge to Public Policy." She draws attention to what is increasingly recognized as the "feminization of poverty." This is not to imply that the impact of unemployment and poverty is less critical for men. Black, Hispanic, and other minority men are suffering serious moral and personal damage from exclusion from the labor market or restriction to marginal, low-paid jobs. Unemployment and underemployment are now serious problems for all groups here and throughout the world. Focus on the feminization of poverty is not meant to divert attention from this reality but rather to highlight new dimensions that have complicated the problem. Kolbenschlag highlights the concentration of poverty among single parent families and children. She speaks of this as a convergence of gender and class in the growing disparity in life chances. One could add to this the place of generational disparity, since the growing poverty in the United States and throughout the world is having its most telling impact on the younger generation as well as on the women who have usually carried major responsibility for children. Some social critics have noted that the emergence of an impoverished younger generation is a distinctive feature of our new era. Madonna Kolbenschlag speaks of this as "a unique historical crisis," and urges immediate and major interventions.

Jonathan Kozol's study of homeless families, again mostly single mothers and children, in rat-infested dilapidated hotels in Manhattan gives further details.[1] Women were forced to go out daily in search of work and residence without sufficient funds or resources to obtain them. Children were cooped up in small spaces amid drugs and prostitution, violence and decay. A Cuban pastor expressed very well the appalling character of such urban poverty on a visit to Trenton, New Jersey, in the 1980s. He said he had never seen such poverty. It made him wonder which country was underdeveloped, Cuba or the United States.

Kolbenschlag and Kozol are drawing attention to problems that beset the organization of work today. These problems may vary in intensity from one society to another, but the difficulties are endemic to the global system of market exchange and capital accumulation. There are, of course, many forms of this system of accumulation, from corporate capitalism to state organized capital accumulation. In all cases, however, the power is located at the center of the hierarchical system of control. Those on the margins or periphery, whether individuals, families, or whole countries, are exploited for the benefit of the center. Whether under the name of socialism or free enterprise or communism, capitalism is the system that now dominates the production and distribution of goods throughout the world.

The capitalistic system, in its corporate or state form, uses human labor to produce commodities, build capital, accumulate markets, and gain profits. The system is constructed to exploit all the elements that enter into productive and reproductive life. The capitalistic system operates at its most efficient when it has access to the cheapest labor, resources, and land; it flourishes when it can control all of these elements and the markets to which it distributes its commodities. The larger the pool of cheap labor, the lower its labor costs; consequently, little is gained in the system by raising the standard of life for the poorer sectors of the society. The key word in this system is control of the elements of production. The goal is maximum profit and accumulation of capital. As capitalism moved into the high-tech era, it was able to mechanize many of its operations and reduce the costs for labor. This paved the way for a secondary labor market of marginal employment and underemployment in service areas. It is to this market that most women as well as minorities have been shunted. The keynote in the emergence of capitalism has been exploitation of the most vulnerable sectors of the society. This included women and children in the earlier stages. It now includes women and minorities, though increasingly white males are caught in this secondary labor market. In this respect, our economic crisis is not new or unique. We have simply shifted from one vulnerable group to another. It is always the most vulnerable who are the victims of exploitation: African slaves in the seventeenth and eighteenth centuries; African men, women, and children in the twentieth century; Latin American peasants since the colonization of the New World. Always the most vulnerable, those most easily subjected to control, become victims of exploitation. This is not to deny the vaunted productivity of this system, but only to highlight its costs in human life and work, which continue to be enormous.

Returning to Kolbenschlag's claim of uniqueness, however, it can also be argued that we are now encountering a new and difficult condition in the expansion of the capitalist world. The erosion of communal bonds, which we have considered, is now revealing its ugly side. Families are sustained by communal systems of support. When communal life erodes, these support systems dwindle and even disappear in many cases. This means that women and children are caught up in the grinding wheels of capitalistic exploitation of labor. Women and children have always been caught in the system, of course, whether as cheap labor or as the reproductive system that provided workers and cared for them. However, now the reproductive system is directly enmeshed with the search for cheap labor. In fact, the poverty and marginal labor of single mothers means that the whole reproductive system is now placed in jeopardy. The future of a whole generation of children is clearly threatened by inadequate nutrition, faulty preparation for school life, lack of after-school care, and disruption of ordinary home life. The exploitative force of the productive system now impinges destructively on the future of the reproductive process in the society.

Despite the deepening interdependence of life in a high-tech world, our relationships in families, neighborhoods, localities, and even nations become more and more distant. The homeless families in Manhattan, for example, as Jonathan Kozol has shown, are hidden away from sight and perish in anonymity. Ghetto life in our cities is set apart from major business and shopping areas. It becomes an invisible world of unknown suffering and violence. Impoverished older folk are stashed away in the attics of the gray areas of cities. Families are fragmented by the disruptive forces of unemployment, inadequate income, or welfare policies that penalize couples who remain together. In short, the concentration of economic life on production at any price means that the bonds of family, neighborhood, local community, and even national life are eroded. We are inheriting the whirlwind that has been created by generations of single-minded attention to accumulation and profit. The most vulnerable are always the victims of such decay. These are the women and children who remain as the remnants of a devastated familial and communal life.

We could call this a crisis in the generative capacities of our society. Erik Erikson used the term "generativity" in his studies of personal development to designate the capacity to bear and care for the next generation. He considerd this a sign of maturity in the growing adult. He did not mean that everyone had to have children or even want to bear children and assume the role of parent. He meant rather that maturity involved the capacity to assume responsibility for the next generation, whether in parenthood or in caring for society as a whole or even in concerning oneself with the natural environment. This, at least is the way in which I understand his profound concern for the generative capacities of a person. Using this category, we can identify our present crisis as one of generativity.

Men and women are producing children and, for the most part, trying to care for them, although they are under great stress in the deprived sectors of the society. At the same time, the organization of work is undermining the generative capacities of the society as a whole. Whatever the women in the hotels for the homeless may try to do, societal forces and public policies undermine their efforts. If one assumes that a people's reproductive capacities as well as productive life are decisive for their future, then we are indeed in a critical period in the life of the Republic.

Justice, as we noted earlier, is the structure of mutuality through which the moral web of personal and communal life is sustained. Justice, in this basic sense, means that the worth and needs of persons, as well as their freedom, are sustained by the organization of the society. In this sense, the crisis of generativity is an indicator of radical injustice in the organization of contemporary society. Reproductive life requires basic conditions of stability in familial and communal life in order to carry out its obligations. Care and feeding of the young cannot be left merely to chance. Proper nutrition for mothers, presence of both parents where possible, and adequate housing, food, clothing, and health care are minimal essentials for reproductive life. Justice requires that the reproductive needs of a people are respected and supported.

We are at a transitional point in the organization of our productive and reproductive system. The financial needs of families have made it necessary for both parents to work outside the home in most cases. Where work is marginal, it is almost impossible to maintain a family even with both parents working outside the home. Hence, the breakdown in the organization of productive work is undermining the reproductive vitalities of the whole society. Productive injustice is the denial of basic opportunities to use our skills and capacities in maintaining life. Reproductive injustice is the denial of the conditions necessary for the healthy survival of the society. We are clearly at a difficult point in the development of high-tech societies. We are suffering a critical convergence of destructive forces in both the productive and reproductive fields of work. The obvious way through this difficult situation is a communal reorganization of work and the development of a stable environment for the fulfillment of familial work.

Many important steps can be taken to relieve the immediate suffering of parents and children. Creating welfare policies that build respect and opportunity, making decent low-cost housing available, and providing adequate health and educational services—these and many other steps can relieve the worst effects of the crisis for the moment. However, the more basic question is the organization of work within and outside the home. This means building the moral fabric of life in community and workplace. No amount of handwringing over drugs and violence in the streets can replace these basic needs of all people. People need opportunities to grow in stable communities where work is available and parents and surrogates can be available for care. A productive system that promises plenty and fails to meet such basic needs has simply failed its people. At the very best, this suggests that our present crisis requires a communal reorganization of our productive and reproductive work.

The Meaning of Work
Work has been so completely taken over by the labor markets that we tend to think of work as something apart from

ordinary personal life. Children think of their parents as going off to "work." Parents tell their children that they will see them in the evening after "work." Wives are more and more engaged in the labor market; one commonly speaks of them as "working wives." When this understanding of work is accepted, as it has been in the industrial age, the unemployed are simply those who are not working. Work is thought of as something that one may or may not have. In the same sense, industry invented retirement as a point in life when one ceased "working," since this fitted the intention of industry to mobilize labor as an element of production and dispose of labor at the point when it was no longer efficient or useful. Retirement is taken to mean that one is no longer working. Thus, work became labor, and labor fell under the thrall of industrial management. The only work that was recognized or rewarded was the labor that served the industrial and agricultural projects of the high-tech society. Certainly, farm families were never deceived by this removal of work from everday life, for the productivity of a farm depends upon the work of all family members throughout their lives. However, agribusiness has displaced more and more of the family farms, transforming farm work into part-time labor in planting, cultivating, and harvesting.

The meaning of work, once it is liberated from the mentality of an industrial system, has to do with who works, what rewards work may bring, and how work is organized. We have stressed language and communication in the interpersonal networks of personal life. Consequently, we have postponed consideration of the crucial place of doing and making. Speech brings much that we do and feel to the level of explicit meaning, but many feelings and thoughts find expression in gestures, facial expressions, shrugs of the shoulders, postures, and the subtle ways in which we move and work. We acknowledge the place of action in communication in the saying, "actions speak louder than words." In this sense, our doing and making reveal who we are as much or more than do our words. Our speech communicates our feelings and thoughts to others, and actually to ourselves, since we often know what we think only after we have put our thoughts into words. At the same time, our actions and gestures exemplify our way of being with things and others, revealing much that we may not even realize ourselves. How often people who are close to us comment on our moods or attitudes from observing us, sometimes before we are even aware of our feelings. We are beings of language and discourse. We are at the same time beings of bodily actions and movement. Our world is shaped by the interplay between these two aspects of our way of being as persons. A world without words would not be a human world, because its meanings would never be raised to the level of consciousness. On the other hand, a world only of words would be an abstract and barren world, concealing much of our feeling and sensibility. Discourse is, of course, a kind of action, but its full richness only appears through the bodily exchanges that often say more than words.

Doing and making are the working that is so integral to our being as persons and communities. In making this claim, we are enriching the understanding of work and beginning to remove it from the control of the labor markets. At the risk of giving too broad a meaning to work, we can best understand ourselves and our communities by recognizing that communal life is a work. It is an artistic creation through speaking, caring, expressing, doing, and making. The networks of community in which we live, many of which are handed on to us by former generations, are brought into being and maintained by the daily work of people. Families come to be through the work of parents in communicating and providing, cleaning and nurturing, disciplining and supporting. They are also created by the responses of the children to the parents, to one another, to their peers, and to their whole world. A family is "produced" in the best sense of that word through the shared work of all of its members, even as the human species is reproduced through the work of families and the communities that help to sustain them. It may seem strange to call this "artistic creation," for we tend to restrict the term *art* to the fine arts of painting, sculpture, music, and poetry. However, the fine arts are intense expressions of human capacities for communicating and reshaping the world of nature and human relationships. Even as a poem or a novel is a work wrought through the skill of the poet or novelist, bringing an infant to maturity is a work of patience and sensitivity that draws on the creative capacities of parents, siblings, and friends.

We humans are workers, and perhaps all living forms are workers in different ways. In the human case, we bring communities into being, even as communities bring persons into being. We nurture and sustain our common life through our actions and words, sometimes undermining them through our greed and bad faith. This work of community building, relying as it must on the moral texture of relationships, is the foundation on which industries, schools, governments, and other institutions rest. The patient work of the couple in the mom-and-pop store, the hard work of the trash collector, the tedious work of the teacher correcting papers at the end of a long day, the worker cleaning his machine before closing down, the police officer patrolling on foot or by car, the secretary at the word processor, the manager at the telephone, the researcher in the laboratory, the nurse at the ward desk or bedside—all of these human capacities, skills, and energies build and maintain, produce and reproduce, a shared world, a network of personal and communal life.

The conversion of work into labor in industrial society led to major increases in production. The division of labor, the marketing of labor as a commodity, the removal of work from the household, and the transformation of labor, resources, and land into elements for production—this total process that Karl Polanyi called "The Great Transformation"—paved the way for the productive society of accumulation. Enormous human and natural energies were mobilized for production, extending the search for resources and markets throughout the world. Our complex society is the result of several centuries of this development. Its benefits and deficits are a consequence of displacing work from its communal context and incorporating it within the capital market. Whatever our judgments on the values of this historical transformation, there is no way to undo what has been done. We now live in the complex world of massive organizations, which this system created. We are bound to one another through the exchanges of a global market. It is a market that benefits some and injures others. Maximizing the benefits while overcoming the difficulties will depend upon the degree to which we can recover the meaning of work and its communal context.

When work became a commodity, its communal character was obscured. In a market society, each individual is presumed to contract independently for his or her labor. That contract is supposed to be determined by the individual's interests. It does not in fact work that way, for most people seek such work as they can find and hope to manage with it. However, the market principle creates the illusion that work is a strictly individual proposition. This is actually a fiction, for we are bound together in our work and sustain one another through all of our exchanges. This moral and communal quality of work is hidden by the mechanism of the market, for each individual seems to be prospering or failing on his or her own merits. In fact, the whole community is advancing or regressing on the basis of its common work. This community of work is the moral infrastructure of a viable society.

Much has been made of individual liberty in the market. The idea is that the market provides individuals with choices, both in one's line of work and in bargaining for wages or salary. There is truth in this claim, since market capitalism emerged from a feudal era in which most people were bound to the soil or to the work in which they were nurtured. However, work in a high-tech society is anything but a field of liberty. The industrial and other institutional enterprises of our society are organized in very authoritarian patterns. The major realm of liberty now is the private life-style of those who earn enough to enjoy some of the privileges of the consumer society. Individual liberty is a very constricted field in a high-tech society.

Personal liberty, as we argued earlier, cannot be separated from the capacity to maintain and build relationships. Liberty is very much a matter of the quality of communal life and the affirmation of persons within that life. Moreover, as we observed, liberty involves judging, deciding, and choosing in the matters that are important to one's life. When work became a commodity, its participatory character was removed. Workers had no voice in the matters pertaining to their work. This has nothing to do with whether their earlier condition had allowed liberty in work, since the issue is whether work as a commodity is liberated work. Our work is our way of contributing to the total life of a community, however limited our tasks and abilities. The liberty of work is the range of responsibility that persons and communities can assume for those contributions. The authoritarian system of organizing work, however effective it may have been in the earlier stage of industry, no longer fits the realities of an educated society. It removes liberty rather than enhancing it. Moreover, it undermines community rather than enabling persons to learn their responsibilities as contributors to the well-being of the community.

I am proposing that how we work with and for one another, as well as for ourselves, builds or erodes the moral fabric of our common life. Work is, in this sense, what Alasdair MacIntyre calls a "practice."[2] He does not, in fact, view most work as a practice, since he means by practice a cooperative human activity in which the doing is its own reward. For example, a practice would be a game like chess or an artistic endeavor or a scientific inquiry. His main point is that practices involve rules and standards that are inculcated as we engage in a practice. For example, we follow the standards of a proper science in carrying through our experiments and reporting our findings. The goods or benefits of such a practice are, in his view, the sheer joy of discovery, or, in the case of a game, the pleasure of the game. He is concerned with the way in which a practice builds character and virtue by training us in the disciplines of the game or art or science.

This notion of practice is too valuable to confine to the region of such select activities. MacIntyre would probably be willing to admit that all activities involve both internal and external rewards, although there will be differences in emphasis. Certainly, skill in a game gives pleasure in the game but also a sense of worth and achievement. The same would be true in scientific work or artistic creation. Whether the work be science or medicine or nursing or raising children or making a tool in a factory or teaching a class, work gives a sense of being able to do something. We can grant that many kinds of work bring very little in the way of personal, internal rewards, though even here we can note the depression that comes with unemployment or the failure to find work. Hence, we can properly carry over MacIntyre's notion of practice to all fields of work, arguing that all work should provide internal and external rewards. Like any practice, work follows rules and standards, and those criteria should build character and virtue, making us better citizens. Work is, in this sense, an exemplification of the best qualities in the society's self-understanding of its moral life. Work is the occasion for building communities and personal worth. If, by contrast, work is organized as a commodity and shaped to control the workers, appealing only to their selfish interests in order to keep them in line, then work has become a hindrance to the building of a moral community. Rather than building community, work then becomes a source of decay within the common life. As MacIntyre puts it,

> We should therefore expect that, if in a particular society the pursuit of external goods were to become dominant, the concept of the virtues might suffer first attrition and then perhaps something near total effacement, although simulacra might abound.[3]

Practices are, in fact, organized in institutional networks. This is as true of a chess game as of a scientific inquiry. Chess games usually take place in informal contexts, yet they involve a matrix of expectations and values. One does not bring the chessboard into surgery or to the assembly line. Whatever the activity, certain standards operate and specific contexts are considered appropriate. Institutions may be rather informal, yet they shape the rules and values that are at play in particular activities.

The interplay between practice and institution reveals the way in which cultural values and beliefs are enacted in the institutional life of a society. The organization of work inculcates basic virtues or vices, inscribing certain values in the practices of daily life. Alasdair MacIntyre is on good ground in raising questions about the moral future of a society in which institutions celebrate greed and personal advantage. No amount of personal goodwill can substitute for the standards of life that are embodied in our institutional life. In this sense, change comes about in a society only when new values and concerns penetrate the major institutions that govern daily life. Cultural values and institutions are not synonymous, but they are interwoven in every aspect of the common life, just as mind and body interact in every moment of life.

The Spirit of Institutions

Although we make the distinction between culture and institution, we recognize that institutions are organizations of culture, even as culture is the linguistic and symbolic expression of institutional life. In this sense, we employ the two terms only in order to identify important aspects of a people's way of life. Culture and institutions are two sides of the same coin. The unifying reality is a people's way of being in the world; their manner of living, acting, and thinking; their ways of loving, working, and deciding.

Separation of culture and institutions is a common fault in the thinking of social critics. If they focus simply on cultural expressions in literature and education, they obscure the ways in which a people's action shapes its cultural life. If they focus only on economic and political processes, they reduce thought to a mere excrescence of financial negotiations or political strategies. Benjamin Barber challenged this "culturism" on the part of authors who, like Allan Bloom, criticize our youth and our educational system as though students and institutions operated in an ethereal realm of pure mind. Barber drew attention to the fact that forty-seven-year-olds operated pretty much in the mental climate of the seventeen-year-olds who were being criticized. Then he observed,

> We honor ambition, we reward greed, we celebrate materialism, we worship acquisitiveness, we commercialize art, we cherish success and then we bark at the young about the gentle arts of the spirit. The kids know that if we really valued learning, we would pay their teachers what we pay our lawyers and stockbrokers. If we valued art, we would not measure it by its capacity to produce profits. If we regarded literature as important, we would remove it from the celebrity sweepstakes and spend a little money on our libraries.
>
> Kids just don't care much for hypocrisy, and if they are illiterate, their illiteracy is merely ours, imbibed by them with a scholarly ardor. They are learning well the lesson we are teaching—namely, that there is nothing in all the classics in their school libraries that will be of the slightest benefit to them in making their way to the top of our competitive society.[4]

However, the question still remains as to how a pattern of action communicates a moral and spiritual reality. Practices are things that are done in particular ways. By contrast, ideas, images, stereotypes, and symbols are ways of thinking and seeing, understanding and perceiving. We have a common saying, "actions speak louder than words." The question that arises in the organization of work is precisely how racist actions and institutions do in fact speak. How do practices embody meanings in such fashion that we cannot change our cultural life without dealing directly with our institutions? How can we take seriously the criticisms of our educational life without dealing with the total way of life that confirms or subverts it?

We gain insight into this interplay of culture and institution by considering the linguistic character of human life that we have discussed previously. We humans bring the rhythmic energies of life, the bodies and things of the world, into webs of meaning through a metaphoric process. Our creative, artistic way of being is to fashion a world of meaning from rhythmic flows of energy that are not yet meaning. Our metaphoric linguistic disclosures are better and poorer expressions of the rhythmic flow of natural and personal life. They are always open to improvement. Although we never fully capture the infinitely complex flow of these rhythms, our linguistic strategies do enable us to cope with our world, and our metaphoric innovations constantly expand the everyday world of meanings. A poet refers to the "temple of nature." The Reagan administration refers to mercenary terrorists whom it has hired in Central America as "freedom fighters." Paul tells the Corinthians that they are "the body of Christ." Whether to abuse our minds, as with the idea of "freedom fighters," or to enrich our spiritual life, as in the image of "the body of Christ," metaphors disclose a world that is ever new and challenging. This is familiar ground for most of us, since we live in and through our linguistic discourse, and we enjoy the innovative power of metaphoric insights.

However, practices are also events that bear meanings. They illumine and confuse, revealing and concealing our way of life. Most of our action, like our discourse, is filled with meanings that we take for granted. Our eating, working, sleeping, playing, and resting follow routines that we only think about when the food is bad or the tool breaks or we cannot get to sleep. These are linguistic activities only in the sense that we make sense of them through language, and we understand them, when we have to, by thinking about them in linguistic terms. If we meet a friend in the morning who groans about difficulty in sleeping, we understand that this was a bad night. In a similar way, the separation of white and nonwhite people conveys a certain meaning that can be uncovered with reflection.

If our actions, and thus our institutional patterns of acting, are bearers of linguistic meanings, they are also metaphoric events. This follows simply from the fact that linguistic meanings arise through metaphoric processes of tensive transformation in which taken-for-granted meanings yield new disclosures. However, we know that a gesture or way of sleeping is not itself a verbal linguistic event. The question is, What kind of a metaphoric event is an action, and especially a patterned action that dramatizes relationships between groups of people? What kind of metaphoric event is the competitive practice that conveys to the young person that there is no point in wasting time on classical literature if he or she wishes to make a killing in the market? If we can comprehend the metaphoric quality of action, we gain some insight into the meaning of the adage, "actions speak louder than words," for the implication is that actions bear meanings with an even more powerful impact than verbal expressions.

Paul Ricoeur offers some insight into this metaphoric quality of practice in a series of studies titled, *The Rule of Metaphor*. He proposes that we try to grasp how a painting may convey a mood and an insight through what Nelson Goodman calls *exemplification*. Ricoeur notes that a painting may be dark and gray, and may metaphorically possess a sad quality. This brings to mind some of the dark paintings from the latter part of Marc Rothko's life that communicate a deep pathos and a sense of ending. It is not simply that the color, design, and texture create a particular sensibility in the viewer. The painting may not make the viewer sad (though it may), yet sadness is in the painting. As Goodman and Ricoeur observe, the painting possesses a specific quality through its composition, giving it a metaphoric property of disclosure. This quality is communicated to the viewer, because it is borne by the painting. The metaphoric process in a painting is an importation of meaning through color, texture, and design, capturing rhythmic flows of energy in which the viewer participates through his or her own being. A painting is not a linguistic expression, yet it bears interpretable meanings and moods. We can speak of the pathos and sadness in the painting. We can feel and discern it. There is an exemplification of meaning in the painting that conveys this sensibility. Through color, composition, and textures, the painter exemplifies meaning and mood.

Actions, practices, and institutional patterns of conduct exemplify moods and meanings in a way similar to that of artistic works. We have already noted that we humans are artistic beings, that our actions and works as well as our cultural expressions are creative, artistic unfoldings of the meaning of our world. Our actions are filled with meaning and convey moods of various kinds. Parents may exemplify love and concern for their children in the way they hug them or keep their distance, often sharing more of their real feelings in their actions than in their words.

If we are to understand ourselves as a people, we face the task of decoding the meanings that are exemplified in our political, economic, and social institutions. Our ideals and hopes are embodied in these patterns of daily life. Our institutions constitute a text that we can read if we are willing to examine them. Thus, an artistic understanding of human life recognizes the interweaving of culture and institutions in the shaping of our common life. We live our values in the way we organize our lives.

Who Controls Work?

The question of the organization of work has become a critical matter for many groups in recent years. Several of the major denominational bodies have produced documents that are extremely critical of the present economic system. The coalition of urban bishops of the Episcopal Church proposes a major program for the churches to explore questions of hunger, unemployment, and practices in work. The catholic bishops issued a pastoral letter on the economy, proposing that our country embark on an experiment in economy that would be comparable to the American experiment in political democracy. In their pastoral, they point to the moral issues that are raised by our economic situation, stating,

> . . . Our faith calls us to measure this economy, not only by what it produces, but also by how it touches human life and whether it protects or undermines the dignity of the human person. Economic decisions have human consequences and moral content; they help or hurt people, strengthen or weaken family life, advance or diminish the quality of justice in our land.[5]

In a similar vein, the coalition of Episcopal bishops made a report to the church at large, stating,

> . . . religiously sensitive people who along with others are getting vocal in advocating the restructuring of economic decision making so that wealth produced by the common efforts of the many will benefit the many and not just the few. Through collective action, often spurred by ecumenical coalitions, neighborhoods are being sustained and restored. Such types of witness are "sacramental signs" that once again our national wealth can become our commonwealth.[6]

These are only two recent statements of concern over an issue that has troubled the human conscience for centuries. Perhaps the most troubling aspect of the present organization of work is the increasing percentage of marginal or low-paid service jobs that are replacing conventional work in the so-called primary labor market. Moreover, much unemployment has come from technical changes in work, in addition to the displacement of industrial work to foreign countries as companies searched for cheap labor. The technologizing of work has come about partly in an effort to reduce costs, but much of it flows from the principle that "if we can, we should." The net effect has not always been beneficial. John Raines and Donna C. Day-Lower describe how the faulty signals at the Three Mile Island nuclear plant confused the operators, since the technical design had bypassed the skills of the workers.[7] Rather than enabling the operators to use their intelligence to control the problems, the automated processes confused them and crippled their efforts. A similar argument has been made in a study by the Brookings Institute, as reported in *The New York Times*, May 3, 1987. The study observed that there are dangers inherent in the computerized technology of recent nuclear weaponry insofar as it bypasses the human intelligence that has proved to be the only factor which has prevented several false alerts from initiating nuclear attacks. These observations raise a broader problem of technical change in work. Whether one ascribes to "small is beautiful" or not, technical innovations in work should be concerned with building human skills and communal life as well as increasing productive efficiency. The principle should be, If we can, we may, and, then again, we may not. We must consider more than short-term efficiency or profit.

These questions about the organization of work are not meant in a simply negative way, for there are many virtues in the present system that need to be carried forward into any new economy. However, questions must be raised. Most of the people in the United States are very conscious of the economic disaster that now plagues the Soviet Union. At least they know this by report and even by statements which Gorbachev himself has made. However, these same people find it difficult to raise serious questions about their own economy, usually for fear that this will categorize them as disloyal or unpatriotic. But the organization of work is a human creation. Every such system has its strengths and its weaknesses. At present, the deficits far outweigh the benefits for more and more people.

The most pressing question about the organization of work is who controls the economy. Where is true power located in the organization of our common work? We argued earlier that power is the shared energy of life in which all people participate. People may vest this power in representatives for particular purposes, but those agents are accountable to them. This is the principle that governed the thinking of the founders of the Republic. They were not willing to settle for a king. They wanted their rulers to be representative of and accountable to the people. Many of our presidents have found this accountability a burden, but each time that they tried to reject it, they have been brought to judgment. On the other hand, in our market economy the organization of work is neither representative nor accountable. The work of the people has gradually been expropriated by corporate powers. Moreover, these powers are not accountable to the people; in fact, in many cases they are not even accountable to a sovereign state. Many of them are actually sovereign powers in their own right with greater wealth than many small nations. The issue confronting anyone who desires to reconsider the organization of work is what it would mean to liberate such an economy. However, before considering this basic issue in the next chapter, we can gain a deeper understanding of the resistance to change in the economy if we consider some of its religious dimensions. There is a religious commitment supporting this economy. This is the source of difficulty in raising questions about economic life in the United States. The economy is the nearest thing that we have to a golden calf.

The Economy as Idol

Many years ago, R. H. Tawney wrote an important critique of the capitalistic system titled, *The Acquisitive Society*. He drew attention to the exaltation of greed in the system, its promotion of what MacIntyre calls external rewards. Perhaps the acquisitive economy would have done less damage to the common life if it had been possible to insulate the market from other sectors of life. However, the cultivation of selfish habits gradually erodes the fabric of community, undermines the virtues that sustain the moral life, and finally creates an institutional life that corrupts personal life. Accumulation becomes a reigning force in all walks of life, whether it be accumulation of consumer goods or capital or wealth or property. A whole society becomes oriented to the increase of its gross national product. Possessiveness, devotion to holding one's goods or capital, becomes the ruling commitment of the people and the principal task of the state. In this way, the possessive society is born. It is a society devoted to retaining what it controls, walling itself in with more and more sophisticated weaponry, celebrating its economic growth year by year. Thus, possessions become an addiction, exerting more and more power over the lives of the people. Those who lose in the zero-sum game are discarded. Those who win cut themselves off from any contact with the losers. Lazarus can no longer appear at the gate, because the gate has become a wall. The possessive society is born from the acquisitive system.

Possession and accumulation became ultimate values in this capitalistic world. Max Weber once observed that three basic motives seemed to drive peoples throughout history: health, wealth, and salvation. If there is some truth in this, wealth became the primary driving force in the Western world. This religious commitment (and what else is faith than one's ultimate commitment?) is so taken for granted that we do not think of it as religious. In fact, the term *secular* became a way of concealing the faith in possessions. Modern society was claimed to be secular or nonreligious, that is, merely concerned with everyday matters and lacking in religious conviction. However, the secular ideology concealed the ultimate quality of Western commitment to accumulation. One can understand that this idea of the secular was spurious, since the secular society of the United States was at the same time burgeoning with confessional bodies and denominations. Confessional faith and devotion to possessions seemed to fit harmoniously into the same world. Somehow faith in God and trust in possessions were reconciled.

In many ways, the triumph of the possessive society has really been a victory of individualism over communalism. Whatever truth and value individualism holds, and it certainly promoted important values of human rights and civil liberty, its total effect was to relegate large sectors of vulnerable people to despair and death. The holders of power increased their control, and the powerless were driven into apathy and silence. Most important, the deeper bonds of working and loving were sundered. The communal character of work eroded. Those who succeeded in work became increasingly insulated from those who most desperately needed their concern and support. Meanwhile, the major institution in which love is sustained, family life, became a victim of productive forces that were oriented only to profitable production. The communal network has always kept human life both human and moral. It has also kept work oriented to the well-being of the whole people, sustaining them in difficult times and giving them cause to celebrate when times were good. This network, the very fabric of loving, was gradually torn away from the organization of work. To be sure, the separation of loving from working never succeeded. Men and women find their fellowship with workmates.

This is still one of the few internal goods they receive in working as well as one of the great losses they suffer with unemployment or retirement. However, the broader communal support for work and family life decayed as work became a commodity in the market. Individuals won or lost in the zero-sum game. Production became a law unto itself. It became the ruling god of the Western world.

When we appreciate the power of this economic Leviathan, we find it difficult to conceive of moving toward a more communal organization of work and common life. However, political life is still to some degree independent of the Leviathan, even though it has been deeply penetrated by economic interests. In the final analysis, the future of loving and working comes down to the political organization of power and decision. Moreover, there is profound discontent with the damage that is being done by unrestrained possessiveness. Much of this discontent is expressed in a kind of quiet despair about the future, yet it reflects a hope that our common life can be more than it is. Meanwhile, the global reach of suffering impinges more and more directly on our daily lives. We cannot escape the reality that people are dying throughout the world from hunger and disease even as we preoccupy ourselves with our gross national product and national debt. Furthermore, as we noted at the beginning of this chapter, we now face a whole generation of young people who have been deprived of basic necessities. We are experiencing a crisis in our generativity as a people, our capacity to nurture the coming generation. We know that the suffering of women and children is an inexcusable travesty in our rich land, one which we can deal with politically if we will. These are the kinds of concerns that can spark a serious political movement to reorganize our life of work so that it can strengthen our moral communal life rather than undermine it. This political task of forging a truly communal age can no longer be postponed.

Chapter Five
A Politics of
Community Building

When we consider political responsibility for the organization of work, we confront one of the most puzzling contradictions in high-tech societies. The citizens of the United States and much of the Western world are beneficiaries of one of the wealthiest, if not the wealthiest, system of production in the history of humankind. At the same time, from thirty-three to thirty-four million people in the United States are living in poverty, though that figure could be increased under different criteria. Moreover, while the United States represents roughly 6 percent of the world's population, it is generally estimated that we consume 40 percent of the world's resources. Despite this enormous consumption of global resources, the productive system is not even feeding its own people; or, at least, it is feeding some very well and starving or impoverishing many others. For a century or more Western powers have organized their work for maximum efficiency and profitability. "Efficiency" in this sense means maximum productivity at minimal cost in labor and equipment. This is a very narrow interpretation of efficiency, since it aims simply at the success of the industry in the market and ignores the well-being of the community in which it operates. Hence, the contradiction grows through the very efficiency that should eliminate poverty and hunger. The great machine of production does not feed its own people, not to speak of the millions of people throughout the globe whom it condemns to landless destitution.

It is sometimes argued that this is not really a contradiction in the life of the United States, since our standard of living is so high that even our poorest citizens are comfortable relative to the rest of the world. This may be true for those in modest circumstances, but it does not hold true for the poorest in our society. One index of serious poverty is the extent of hunger in a society. Hunger, in turn, can be measured by infant mortality, since the rate of death of very young children increases markedly with inadequate food and nutrition for pregnant women and infants. Hunger means chronic shortage of basic nutrients. It was estimated in 1985 that twenty million people were hungry in the United States, and the situation was worsening. J. Larry Brown summarizes the effects of this condition on infant mortality as follows:

> . . . A nation's infant mortality rate [the number of babies per 1,000 live births who die before their first birthday] is widely accepted as a meaningful indicator of the society's general health status. By this measure, the U.S. does not do well compared with other industrialized nations. Its infant mortality rate of 11.2 places it 18th in the world. Japan, Sweden and the U.K. are among the countries that do better. Spain and Hong Kong also outdo the U.S.[1]

He notes further that nonwhite infant mortality in the United States, as one would expect from our racist patterns, is higher than that in Cuba and Jamaica, notably poorer countries. Following the usual pattern of blaming the victim, it is sometimes argued that this malnutrition is a consequence of ignorance about good nutrition. As Larry Brown notes, there is evidence that poor people actually buy more nutritious food than the rest of the population.

Hunger may occur for various reasons. In a productive society like the United States, there seem to be several factors. The most obvious is the lack of public provision for those in need. This includes children in school, pregnant women, and infants, among others. Since 1980 the provision for the needy has been radically reduced. Everything from nutritional and medical care for pregnant women to food stamps and school lunches has been cut to the barest minimum. More fundamental in the long run is the high level of unemployment that is taken for granted: usually said to range from 6 to 8 percent, it actually ranges much higher among minorities and much, much higher when one includes those who have given up on the job hunt. When people cannot find work, they cannot provide for themselves. They become dependent upon state programs or simply go without homes or food. A productive society that cannot provide work is not really a "productive" society except in the narrow sense of output of commodities for those with the means to accumulate. A truly productive society would sustain a healthy community with a decent quality of life.

This contradiction within the productive society is even more troubling on the global stage. Market capitalism has spread over the whole globe during the last century. Recently, transnational corporations have gained major control of resources and markets. Hence, the central powers have been able to control prices and exchange rates, transforming third world areas into export platforms for cheap products and dumping grounds for surplus goods from the center.

This is a familiar picture. The less well-known side of the picture is the domination of the food market by the corporate interests of the central powers. Food has become one of the really profitable commodities on the global market. The land of the third world areas has gradually been converted to crops for export. Coffee, sugar, rice, bananas, and other products form the main crops of many of the nations on the periphery of the market system. Consequently, many third world countries are importing basic food for consumption. These imports are priced too high for most poor people. Their families displaced from the land by the development of agribusiness and deprived of income to purchase food, one-half of the children in these areas die before five years of age and one in eight are starving. The conventional wisdom attributes this terrible suffering to deterioration of soil, overpopulation, and ignorance. Whatever small contribution these factors make to the overall picture, the basic reason is the exploitation of these economies by global capitalism in its various forms.

One of the dreams of market capitalism has been a productive system in which scarcity and hunger could be eliminated. Susan George quotes from a document prepared for the World Food Conference by the International Union of Foodworkers in which the foodworkers comment on the emptiness of this dream:

Agribusiness bears a special responsibility for the present food crisis. While food deficits and malnutrition have grown worse during the past ten years, the accelerated growth rate and prosperity of the multinational firms during the same period has been inversely proportional to the increase of scarcity.

This phenomenon is only paradoxical on the surface; the goal of agribusiness is not to increase food resources, nor to contribute to their equitable distribution, nor yet to adapt existing technology to the conditions of particular countries. Their goal is first and foremost to increase their markets and their commercial outlets, to realize maximum production-costs reduction and to increase their profits. This is a truism, but should be made clear, especially in this Conference, where multinationals are spreading their propaganda about their support capabilities to solve the world food crisis.

Food workers of developing countries have long and bitter experience of this capability. There are great numbers of agribusiness workers whose low salaries, substandard housing, poor health and squalid working conditions are such that hunger, malnutrition and undernourishment for them and for their families are commonplace. If so many multinational firms do not even allow their own workers to feed themselves properly, then how can we imagine for a moment that they can bring a decent diet to everyone?[2]

Although Susan George's text is now somewhat dated, all the recent evidence indicates that the situation is actually worse than when she wrote this text.

The domestic and global failures of the organization of work in our world today raise basic questions that cannot be dismissed. One wonders whether the suffering of minorities in the United States is symptomatic of a global condition that flows from the productive system. The growth of third world debt is alone indicative of basic difficulties in the global economic system. One can pile statistics upon statistics and still not deal with the reality that the most vulnerable are suffering from these economic pathologies while the most powerful increase their privileges and wealth. The convergence of gender, class, and race in the economic crisis of the United States combines with postcolonial exploitation to create a domestic and global economic crisis. This situation can only become worse unless some solutions are found. These issues constitute domestic and international political problems whose resolution will alter the public landscape in the coming years. They are not problems that can be left to an invisible hand nor to some supposed laws of exchange. They are problems that fall to the political responsibility of the people of the world.

Democratic Politics

Politics is the most comprehensive activity of human communities. It is the community's work in shaping its history and preserving its common life. There are many agencies of political life, such as state governments, community organizations, and voluntary associations. In recent years, nation states have tended to claim a monopoly of political activity, partly because the sheer complexity of high-tech societies increases the scope of central governments. Air travel creates domestic and global problems of regulation. The production and distribution of various kinds of drugs and medicines require some kind of control. Environmental conditions become dangerous when toxic chemicals and waste products are dumped indiscriminately. The list is endless, and state bureaucracies have grown accordingly, though some of the growth is undoubtedly part of the natural tendency of large organizations to increase their own power. Nevertheless, the political life of peoples is much broader than these institutions. Even under the most dictatorial conditions, rulers hold power only so long as the people grant their consent, whether voluntary or forced. The consent of the people is the final bastion of their political power.

In this broad understanding, politics is the mobilization of a people's power for the preservation and ordering of its common life. It is a people's common work for the "general happiness," as the founders of the Republic were accustomed to call it. Power, as we have already noted, is the exercise of life in mutuality. It is the shared capacity of persons and communities to shape their lives and cope with their problems. The founders of the Republic were loath to invest too much of this communal power in the hands of their elected representatives, since they feared the imposition of royal authority in a new form. However, they realized that trade, foreign policy, defense, civil order, and territorial questions had to be resolved through a central authority. Their plans for a limited government have had to go through significant changes with the emergence of industrial society and the later complexity of a high-tech world. They could not anticipate the enormous concentration of power that would accrue to some of the corporate giants that now control so much of the productive capacity of the nation. Nevertheless, their essential conviction that government should be accountable to the people has proved to be well founded. The problem is how to maintain that vision under these new economic conditions.

A central question in political life is who makes the decisions and how those decisions are made. In a democratic republic, decisions are vested in representatives of the people. Under the rural and mercantile conditions of the late eighteenth century, representatives could be held accountable to local constituencies. As the organization of work became more complex, large financial institutions penetrated the governmental structures. Working with the idea of limited government, these economic powers influenced decisions, gained access to privileges, and generally dominated the political scene. Gar Alperovitz and Jeff Faux call this degradation of political life the emergence of the "broker state."[3] They mean by this term a political apparatus that works to balance the interests of various economic organizations, maintaining their power by distributing contracts and privileges among different pressure groups. So-called "defense" expenditures have accounted for the most dramatic allocation of bounty to industrial giants.

When one reckons with the fact that "preparations for war have cost the United States $2 trillion since 1981," as reported by the Center for Defense Information, then this penetration of political life is appalling. This figure amounts to $21,000 for each household in the United States. This expenditure contributed significantly to the increase in the national debt, which grew from $1 trillion in 1981 to $2.6 trillion in 1987. Clearly, limited government is a fiction under these conditions. The real question is how, if at all, a democratic republic can establish its political responsibility for the common life under these conditions of a high-tech world.[4]

Politics can be and often is corrupted by the expropriation of a community's power by special interests. We have already considered how the possibility of control and domination is a constant temptation to persons and communities. Securing our interests through control over persons or resources seems to stave off the threat of nothingness and death, though in the end it proves self-defeating. However, the exercise of power, our basic political capacity, is not an evil force nor an aberration in the human spirit. The capacity to interpret what is going on, to judge a situation, to choose a course of action, to decide how to proceed—this is the essential human power to affect the world and to assume responsibility for the future. There is a saying in the feminist movement that "the personal is political." This seems a sound insight. Personal life, family relations, community experience—all facets of life are fields for the exercise of power in interpreting, judging, and deciding. We noted in chapter 2 that the women who were making decisions about abortion were often under pressure from husbands, parents, or boyfriends. We also observed that their own decisions were an exercise of power over their own bodies and the fetal life they bore. Humans are political beings. Through their political capacities they can build livable communities or bring endless pain and difficulty to one another. The founders of the Republic seemed to appreciate these capacities and tried to balance the exercise of powers in such a way that none would become preponderant and all would remain accountable to the people. Following their intentions, we now face the task of bringing the economic powers into balance and holding them accountable to the citizenry.

The complex structures of society are built upon the basic capacities of the human being. This does not imply that the organization of work is simply an aggregate of individual efforts. A business or industry is a complex network of relations that organizes human capacities for work into a common enterprise. This organization is always more than its individual participants, just as a family is more than an aggregate of its individual members. A family or a business is a whole that is greater than or more than the sum of its parts. It is a community of its own kind with expectations, systems of reward, rules of operation, and ways of maintaining relationships. At the same time, a family or business works by drawing upon the capacities of members for loyalty, for judging situations, and for working together. The politics of a family have to do with who has authority, ways of supporting one another, ways of protecting one another, and, at their worst, ways of scapegoating certain members. The same holds for an office, a bank, a class in school, or a transnational corporation.

It would be naive to presume that there is a blueprint at hand to overcome these basic problems in the organization of work. But the important fact is that some new approaches are needed. A new direction is imperative for the very survival of millions of people. On the other hand, fear of change is widespread. Many would opt for the evil at hand as preferable to an unknown future. However, the risk of finding a new path really means a willingness to look critically at the pain and suffering that surrounds us. One advantage of such a critique is that the ideologies of market capitalism and communism have lost much of their appeal in most parts of the world. There is disillusionment with the pretentious claims of both of these ideologies, their vaunted promise of freedom, equality, and security. One does not have to fall prey to either of these ideologies in order to begin the difficult task of community building. One only has to be ready to face the *is not* that threatens the human future in our time. This, of course, is a tall order for people who have become addicted to possessions.

If we are to get beyond ideological debate with the dominant views of public order, we shall have to move on a very practical level to consider steps toward rebuilding community life. One point of access on this level is the idea of security. We reject the image of the safety net, since it presupposes that human beings are individuals perched alone on a high wire. This is a false and destructive image of the person, according to our preceding interpretation. An alternative view is one in which persons find some sense of security in the bonds of communal life and the support structures that communities provide. Clearly, some tension has to be maintained between security and freedom, since a completely enclosed community might be very secure but stifling to freedom. Hence, the task is to achieve a reasonable level of security in one's life and work, not a nest in which feeding is done at regular hours. Moreover, security is a central symbol in the global network of relations. In fact, national security is invoked as the single most important value in international relations. However, this invocation of security actually eventuates in a global war system that is bleeding the world. Consequently, community building on a global level will have to reconsider the real meaning and possibility of international security. This is one of the political responsibilities confronting all the nations of the world. It means placing the bonds of loving concern and the communal being of persons at the center of economic and political organization. On an organizational level, this involves building a network of mutuality or justice in our productive and reproductive communities.

A Politics of Work

Political responsibility for community life and work has had low priority in the United States. As we noted above, the idea of limited government implied freedom for trade and industry to develop with minimal restrictions. The economic functions of government were to be the preservation of contracts that protect the market against fraud and force. The gradual extension and complication of industrial development made limited government more a fiction than a reality. The political community gradually became deeply implicated in the organization of work, production, and distribution, if only in its function as a broker state. However, posing the question of security or stability in work and community life raises the question of a more significant role for government. It means that the political bodies would assume an important place in planning for the well-being of persons and communities.

Planning is anathema to much of the business community. It is associated with the centralized planning of the communist and socialist countries, a system that has not been at all successful in Soviet Russia and Communist China. However, there are different kinds of planning. One need not think in terms of centralized planning in order to consider how an economy can provide some stability for business, for persons, for local communities and regions, and for national and international life.

Actually, the United States government is deeply involved in planning through its monetary and fiscal policies. The allocation of income through tax policy distributes economic power throughout the community. Control of the money supply by the Federal Reserve determines who shall prosper and who shall suffer, who shall benefit and who shall sacrifice. The fact is that most of the planning in the United States economy is conducted by the major corporations through their investment policies, plant relocations, takeovers, and union negotiations. There is, as we noted above, indirect planning by corporate agencies through their influence in government and the awarding of contracts. Yet, this planning, such as it is, tends to be ad hoc and usually favors the most influential corporations or interest groups. The net effect is instability in policies and markets, leading to suffering for people and damage to the organization of work.

Any consideration of planning within our society will have to take seriously the problems created by centralized bureaucratic planning. All the evidence points to the tendency of major bureaucracies to become concerned for maintaining their own institutional power; as a consequence, they become less productive and increasingly insulated from their constituencies. This is not a special failing of governmental bureaucracies. Industrial, educational, and other institutions have proved equally ineffective and inaccessible to the public. The miserable failures of the United States auto industry after their successes in the 1950s and 1960s can be partly attributed to this bureaucratic hypertrophy. If planning is to be politically responsible and accountable, it will have to include adequate representation from local communities, workers and management, state and regional bodies, and the agencies of the central government. This implies that planning councils would have to be established in order to formulate policies appropriate to different levels of community life.

A first step toward such a politics of work will have to be strengthening the economic life of local communities. Major efforts have emerged on this level. Community land trusts, housing cooperatives, worker-owned businesses, credit unions, and community development corporations have already demonstrated their values. Some of the confessional bodies have furthered these community developments with considerable success. A crucial problem, however, is the flow of capital that is necessary for such development. Only significant investment by federal agencies and pension funds will make it possible to further such a formation of community responsibility. In itself, these local efforts may not alter the conditions of the national and international economic crisis. However, the building of local and regional communities will be essential to creating a base for democratic planning of a stable and workable economy.

The mobility of capital in national and international pipelines is in many ways the major obstacle to economic development in local communities. There are, of course, advantages in such mobility for the expansion of major corporations, some of it beneficial for the life of work. On the other hand, much of the mobility is manipulated in ways that damage work and community life. Barry Bluestone documents this situation very clearly:

> . . . the sheer amount of employment turnover reflecting capital investment, disinvestment, and mobility is extraordinary. In the country as a whole, between 1969 and 1976, private investment in new business plants [including stores, shops, warehouses, and offices, etc.] created about 35 million jobs, an increase of 50 percent over the 1969 base. This amounts to an average of 5 million jobs created each year as the direct result of plant openings. Presumably this is all to the good.

> The bad news is that, by 1976, shutdowns of existing facilities had wiped out 44 percent of the jobs that had existed in the country back in 1969. A total of 31 million jobs were eliminated by plant closings over the seven year period. This amounts to about 4.4 million jobs destroyed each year, on average. Knowing what was happening in the Northeast—the final gasps of the mill-based industries in New England and the fiscal crises in cities like New York—one is not surprised to see that the number of jobs destroyed in this area of the country exceeded the number created. One might be surprised by the apparent better employment record in the Midwest, but this is explained by the fact that the major auto, steel, and tire plant closings in Michigan and Ohio did not take place until after 1976.[5]

When one is aware that each job lost means ten incomes lost to the community, then the problem of responsible planning of capital allocation becomes a central issue for a politics of work.

Another aspect of the politics of work is the creation of ecologically sound agricultural and industrial production. So long as government is dominated by major corporations, there is little reason to anticipate serious concern for the environment. In the present organization of work, environmental consequences are viewed as externalities or nonbusiness costs by major industries; in other words, they are costs that are relegated to government or local communities. This implies that planning councils will also have to assume responsibility for the impact of economic policies on the environment. This is a far more serious problem than is popularly assumed, although discussions of issues like the ozone layer are beginning to reach a broad public. Nicholas Georgescu-Roegen, who has investigated these problems in terms of entropy, takes a dim view of our willingness to face these issues. He observes,

> . . . Once man expanded his biological powers by means of industrial artifacts, he became ipso facto not only dependent on a very scarce source of life support but also addicted to industrial luxuries. It is as if the human species were determined to have a short but exciting life. Let the less ambitious species have a long but uneventful existence.[6]

One need not be so despairing of the human capacity for foresight and responsibility, yet the evidence thus far indicates that this is a reasonable judgment. It is one more aspect of the erosion of the capacity for generativity that we considered under the rubric of the devastation of the lives of mothers and their children. Local communities are very concerned about the effects on their lives of toxic contamination of water and air, but thus far they have had little voice in shaping national and global economic policies. This would imply that the building of local responsibility and its articulation in major centers of power will be absolutely essential to confronting the ecological crisis that undermines the health and future of our world.

A major obstacle to public planning is our national tendency to relegate questions of value to the market. This is, in fact, an abdication of our values to the marketing skills of major companies and their advertising agencies. There is actually far more public consensus over basic needs than our organization of work recognizes. Most people would agree that decent affordable housing, an adequate amount of nutritious food, an education, a job, accessible transportation, and sufficient energy to maintain one's life are common goods that all should share. These are best understood as public goods in a high-tech world. Unfortunately, they are controlled and distributed for profit by private interests. Planning councils could begin their task of allocating investment funds and furthering various projects to enable communities to produce and share in these public goods. Justice as mutuality presumes the existence of such common values. This still allows considerable room for personal decisions about allocation of resources and determination of residence and work. However, it means that a minimal level of security would be available to everyone. All of this presupposes planning for a more stable organization of our economic life, reducing cycles of unemployment to a minimum, and finding ways to introduce new industries and activities into communities from which obsolete plants have to be removed. Change need not be a problem in community life so long as there are institutions to deal with change and foster healthy personal and communal life.

Global conflict between individualism and collectivism creates much of our difficulty in moving toward a democratic organization of work. Individualistic capitalism is pitted against collective state capitalism in a cold war. Much of this conflict is detached from the real struggles of people. There is much in common between market capitalism and centralized, planned capitalism. Yet, the productive process is organized and directed in both cases by managerial bureaucracies. The corporate managers promote the interests of their corporations and owners. The collective managers promote their own power bases and the interests of their states. In both cases, the needs of people and their democratic engagement in work are overlooked or actually undermined. There is no simple and sovereign remedy for these distortions in the ownership and control of work. Market-oriented economies will continue to develop in ways that preserve the liberties and values of market choices. Our task in furthering the interests of people in such economies is to develop democratic planning in ways that preserve personal rights and opportunities. This will mean realistic criticism of the faults in market capitalism. It also means readiness to acknowledge that criticism is possible without advocating collectivism or centralized, authoritarian planning. We are mature enough as a people to move toward democratic communalism in which shared values and personal rights can live together. This will undoubtedly mean gradual restriction on the arbitrary control of work by those interests that claim ownership of the people's work. However, such restrictions can also be democratically achieved through the cooperative efforts of owners, managers, workers, communities, and governmental agencies. Democratic communalism seems to be the proper direction for overcoming the failures of an empty individualism and a debilitating collectivism.

The problems of economic planning are obviously complicated by the international context in which work, production, and distribution are now operating. Various groups have pursued the question of a global economic order in which stronger and weaker sectors could achieve justice and stability. Some of these efforts have been sponsored by the United Nations and others by the private sector. We are deeply enmeshed in the global market, capital system, and distributive network. The idea of a national economy is significant for maintaining stable work and community life, but it cannot be disentangled from its global context. To this extent, our economic activities have paved the way for the building of global citizenship. In fact, without political efforts to build such citizenship, our economic markets will continue to generate global conflicts and violence. The problem of justice in the world is that of planning a global organization of work to stabilize prices of commodities and allow for local and regional control of economic life. The global problem is not different in kind from the difficulties encountered by local communities within our national context. The difference is only one of scale and a lack of global mechanisms to adjudicate differences without war.

There are international mechanisms for planning, such as the World Bank and the International Monetary Fund, as well as coalitions of the central powers, but there is no adequate mechanism to further the interests of peripheral third world areas in the formation of policies. Quite the contrary, the third world areas are largely pawns in the hands of these major powers. In the long run, progress toward such global planning and justice may arise through recognition of the need for a stable and sustainable world order, one in which availability of land, food, work, and natural resources can be distributed equitably. There will certainly be no end to the terrorism and bloodshed that now scar the international scene until there is justice for those who have suffered exploitation under Western expansion. The high-tech world is now the common heritage of all peoples. The problem of justice is how the work and resources of that world can be shared by all peoples and communities.

In the tradition of a free-market economy, national and global planning are often perceived as undemocratic. The real issue of planning is just the opposite. We have operated much too long with democratic politics and an undemocratic, even authoritarian, planning of work by private interests. We are a relatively educated society, although there is much to be done by way of improving our educational process. Our people are quite prepared to assume responsibility for their economic futures. In fact, we develop our capacities for responsibility only through exercising them. This has certainly been the lesson of the two centuries of the Republic. We are long overdue for the creation of a democratic organization of work and economic policy. However, this will also require the liberation of our political life from its preoccupation with maintaining an outmoded economic system through a global war system. Security in economic life cannot be achieved without some security on a global level; however, there is a difference between a just international community and one in which the United States or the Soviet Union dictates the economic and political terms on which various peoples can survive.

This brings us to the broader problem of politics and security. This is the context in which planning for productive and reproductive justice will have to be developed.

From National to Global Security

Economic forces have influenced United States foreign policy from the outset. Many of the founders were concerned not only with defense of the new federation of states but also with stability in their trading activities. However, economic penetration of political life reached a qualitatively new level after World War II. The United States emerged from that war as the dominant economic, military, and technological power of the world. A war that at first threatened to destroy the United States mobilized its productive energies and technical skills so that its enemies and allies, exhausted or destroyed by the terrible war, no longer rivaled its power. Industry moved into this global vacuum in search of natural resources and future markets. Third world areas were breaking their colonial ties and offered vulnerable regions for this invasion of industry. Meanwhile, Soviet Russia made a remarkable recovery from its wartime devastation, rivaling the United States for domination of the global scene. When Soviet Russia developed its capacity for nuclear weaponry, cold-war rivalry became the setting for all global policies. Out of this witches' brew the national security states were born. It is this phenomenon that now keeps the major states locked in a deadly struggle which may finally be their undoing.

The term *national security state* is usually associated with Latin American nations, governed by military juntas, engaged in covert war against their own peoples, oriented to geopolitical domination of their regions, and organizing themselves in support of private economic interests. These states have brought the military into total hegemony over political and economic institutions. This is especially the case where military aid from the United States has enriched the military elites, as has happened in Honduras, Panama, El Salvador, and Guatemala. In turn, the military has suppressed individual liberties, engaging in the torture and assassination of any liberal groups that seemed to threaten their authority. The horrors perpetrated on the people in Chile, Argentina, Brazil, Guatemala, El Salvador, and in Nicaragua under the Somozas are characteristic of these states.

We do not usually think of the United States as a national security state, since it has the external marks of a democratic republic. However, the United States has been a supporter of these states in Latin America, and in its own way has been on the road to becoming such a state. This tendency in United States democracy emerged largely as a corollary to its engagement in the cold war. The Iran/*contra* scandal was a culmination of an internal conflict in the democracy between the executive promotion of a national security state and the checks and balances of a democratic republic.

Security of borders and interests is certainly a reasonable aim of nation states. There is no question that rivalry with the communist governments of Soviet Russia and later China created a climate in which the United States believed that its capitalistic system was under siege. This sense of threat gave birth to the policy of containment that we associate with John Foster Dulles. That policy was integral to the creation of the national security state. The difficult question is whether this geopolitics of security is a path to real security for the people of the United States as well as for the peoples of this pluralistic world of rich and poor nations, affluent and hungry regions. This is the broader question of whether any nation can be secure in our interdependent world without global security and stability for all nations. Moreover, there is the serious question of whether democracy can survive when a free people becomes a national security state. This latter question of the democratic republic requires serious reflection at this stage in our national life.

The democratic republic is also endangered by engagement in the global war system. This is the Achilles' heel of the national security state. Once a nation embarks on a geopolitical strategy of military action, it corrupts its internal economy and undermines its representative government. The costs of the global war system are now completely out of hand, as Ruth Sivard has made clear in her 1987 report, "Military and Social Expenditures." She notes not only a decline in the United States economy but a spread of military governments as a consequence of United States policies.

> The U.S. gross national product has fallen to 2.2 percent during the 1980s, down from 3.8 percent in the 1960s. In 1986, the amount of money going to the poorest fifth of the population was 4.6 percent, the lowest ever. The wealthiest fifth received 43.7 percent, the highest ever . . .
>
> Fifty-two percent of the 113 nations reviewed in the report are under military control. Sivard noted that 64 percent of the 2.2 million people killed last year in an unprecedented 22 wars

were civilians. The report lists worldwide military spending in 1987 at $930 billion, or $1.8 million a minute.[7]

Corollary to this escalation in militarism is the problem of nuclear weaponry in a democracy. A strategy of nuclear deterrence or massive assured destruction presupposes that there are persons or a person in a position to respond to a nuclear attack by releasing missiles that can annihilate whole regions of the world. Apart from the horror of a military policy built around such indiscriminate annihilation, nuclearism undermines the very basis of a democracy. The role of Congress in representing the people by declaring war is simply canceled by such a strategy. In fact, nuclear weaponry and policy have never come before Congress or the people of the United States in a referendum. The weapons exist, they are stockpiled, and the only possible presumption is that under certain conditions they will be employed. This nuclear strategy on the part of the United States and Soviet Russia means that the peoples of the world are held hostage to a policy of terror.

Militarism is a bad recipe for democracy. Despite contemporary cynicism about the possibilities of international peace, there has to be a better way. Stability in domestic and international economies cannot be built on such military strategies. Security of borders cannot be preserved so long as weapons are freely available to the highest bidders throughout the world. There now exists a global war system in which the profitability of weapons has far outstripped every attempt to preserve a peaceful world. We have indicated above that there is another way to begin thinking about stability for communities in our national and global economies. There also seem to be alternatives to the policies of the national security states for global justice and peace. Certain lines along which such an alternative would proceed can at least be dimly perceived, although the full implications are far from clear at present.

Global Citizenship and Global Community

Although it may seem a strange term to use for a basic shift in national policy, the heart of the matter seems to be a conversion of the people. The present pursuit of security is a religious commitment. It places unconditioned value on defense of the wealth and resources that the major powers have amassed.

This is the real significance of a policy of nuclear warfare in case of attack. The great powers are now obsessed with hanging on to their wealth and power. This applies to most of the central powers in the global economy. The religious belief in national security is impossible to dislodge until people become aware of its self-contradictions and its incredible costs in suffering and human lives. Perhaps this conversion will come only when the suffering strikes at the central powers, but one can hope that an awakening and conversion may come before such a catastrophic event.

This change of heart has to do with the commitment to violence in preservation of wealth and position. Institutional exploitation of peoples, whether at home or abroad, is a strategy of violence. When people are displaced from their lands, thrown out of work, forced from their homes, or abandoned on the streets to go hungry, they are the victims of violence. When they cannot find work or hope and resign themselves to the underground economy of drugs, prostitution, and crime, they are the victims as well as perpetrators of violence. Under these conditions, the privileged sectors charge the victims with violence and terror. They refuse to acknowledge the violence they impose on the victims day by day. Moreover, the strategy of geopolitical domination is inevitably a strategy of violence. It always comes down finally to sending troops, supposedly on maneuvers. The net effect, as we noted, is that a democracy propagated through violence becomes a military dictatorship extending violence. Thus, ideological conflicts in the cold war become violent conflicts and proxy wars imposed on vulnerable peoples throughout the world.

In her book *On Violence*, Hannah Arendt remarked that politics ends when violence begins. Her insight raises real questions about whether a democratic republic can even be a political body if it bases its life and security on violence. However, the inverse of Arendt's insight holds true for the future of our world. The end of violence may be the beginning of politics. Politics in this sense is a dialogue of peoples in an open, shared world. It is commitment to negotiation, compromise, and honest conflicts that do not degenerate into violent struggle. This involves willingness to share in the name of justice and peace, and readiness to hear different claims. This is the open path to democratic communalism both within nations and among the various peoples of our interdependent world. It is the deepest and broadest work of love, the work of building a livable world. It means forgiving past wrongs, learning to live together in this world that becomes smaller and closer year by year. It means surrendering the religion of national security for the only real security that is ever available in this world, the security of mutual trust in justice and peace.

The economic security of the nations on the periphery of the central powers is probably the most important single factor in the building of a just world. This means transforming the system of dependency that has been built upon the global market into a truly interdependent system of exchange. This would mean planning for stability in prices of commodities, enabling peoples on the periphery to build a stable economic life. There is need for regional and global councils to plan for such stable employment and monetary exchange. There is little reason to hope that the established powers will surrender their domination of these markets and their control of third world resources. However, the peoples of these regions can struggle to gain control of their own economies, often having to wrest them from the hands of local elites who operate on behalf of the central powers. The cost of such struggles can be exorbitant, yet the alternative seems to be exploitation and starvation. This implies that a revolutionary struggle for independence is the corollary of emerging steps toward interdependence.

At the point at which these revolutionary movements gain some control of their future, there may be room for councils of nations to begin the process of democratic planning for a healthy organization of work and exchange. However, a major step toward such peaceful resolution will be the conversion of the national security states from a basis of war to one of peace. For the United States, this would mean creating a real strategy of defense in which military power was dedicated to reasonable protection of borders. Clearly this also implies willingness to scale back nuclear capability to an absolute minimum, and preferably to a zero level. There seems to be some readiness on the part of Soviet Russia to discuss such a zero option, whether for economic or military reasons. This does not mean projecting the nuclear field of combat into outer space through a strategy like the Star Wars program. There is no reason to believe that Star Wars is anything more than a transfer of nuclear conflict into space at costs far exceeding anything that is even imagined today.

The heart of the matter is a movement toward a nonviolent world. The very existence of nuclear capability has pointed in this direction since the time of Hiroshima and Nagasaki. There are many signs that various nations would like to see a reduction in the emphasis on military action. The movements toward nuclear-free zones are indicative of a growing awareness that the national security states are simply breeding endless insecurities and dangers. In this sense, the peace movements and antinuclear demonstrations are already creating international theaters for negotiation and exchange. This is also true of the growing ecological concerns for the condition of the oceans, atmosphere, ozone layer, rain forests, and other natural resources. The disaster at Chernobyl (with consequences which are as yet far from clear) brought home to some peoples the dangers to every people of such risky technologies. Voluntary associations, scientific groups, and some political organizations have begun to take seriously the future of life on the planet Earth. This is a far more fragile planet than was assumed in the heyday of the technological revolution. It is now obvious that the environment cannot sustain the stress to which it has been subjected in the last few generations.

The different religious, political, and economic cultures of the peoples in our pluralistic world create conditions under which only open communication and fair exchange can lead to real security, even for the most powerful nations. This is a world of many nations and cultures. No power or superpower can bring such a world into subservient dependence or alignment, although the major powers have attempted to do so in the twentieth century. The path to a just world order can only be one of nonviolent negotiation and willingness to respect differences. That does not come easily to superpowers who are accustomed to imposing their will upon their satellites through military force. However, world security can come only through achieving some common values and interests amid the many differences that characterize our global community. The

United Nations, the World Council of Churches, the ecological and peace movements, and the scientific communities can all contribute to this kind of communication. It means putting aside the global war system and challenging the geopolitics of the national security states, not in the name of some illusory world order but in the name of real global security. We have considerable evidence that such nonviolent struggles for justice can succeed. Mahatma Gandhi's struggle is perhaps the most dramatic, but there are also other witnesses, such as Martin Luther King Jr., Archbishop Romero, Steven Biko, Beyers Naude, and Archbishop Tutu. This is not to say that violence will not occur in struggles for liberation and justice, nor does it imply that every struggle will be crowned with success. It means rather that the powers of love and community can provide the basic framework within which such struggles can proceed toward ultimately peaceful goals.

These pathways toward justice and peace depend upon a vision of a common humanity. Unfortunately, the Western powers have not held a vision of shared humanity in a common world. The two superpowers have vied for superiority in that world, seeking to align various peoples with their own interests. Free market capitalism and collectivist capitalism have not proved helpful in opening the way toward security or justice. Neither ideology has had a vision of a truly pluralistic shared humanity. Both ideologies have fostered the dream of global domination by their own economic and political system. Both are ideologies of possessive societies, committed to the accumulation of wealth and goods for their own peoples, or rather for the elites who control their societies. This is an idolatrous religious vision, as we have argued. It substitutes a closed system of control over resources and lives for an open world of communication. These systems are not communal in any basic sense, for they are systems of domination and exploitation. In this sense, the religious vision of the national security states is a major obstacle to any movement toward world peace.

One cannot seriously call for scaling down the global war system when major powers are committed to accumulation and possessions. Such a system of accumulation requires in the last analysis the violent extraction of resources and wealth from the most vulnerable sectors of nature and humanity. The global war system is simply the inevitable consequence of this struggle to control resources, markets, and peoples. In view of the increasing violence in our world, it may seem quixotic to speak of conversion and of a new global vision of peace and justice. However, the heart of the matter is the deepest commitment of peoples in the central and peripheral powers. It poses the question of commitment: either to perpetuate the global war system or to be willing to turn toward a global community and a broader kind of citizenship. How this commitment enters into the world of politics and decision making is a most complex issue in our time. This brings us back to the question we explored at the outset, the question of the emergence of a religion of the public world as the dynamic of a communal age.

Chapter Six
Religious Transformations

The confessional bodies have a prophetic task in the communal age, a ministry in which some of them are already engaged. For centuries they assumed that Western civilization was the bearer of the world's hope. This is no longer so evident, and there are many indications that it was a false hope. The faith communities of the West lent legitimacy to their royal and democratic sovereignties through most of this period. They generally confined their proclamation and pastoral work to the cure of souls, trusting the political religions to fulfill the divine mandates for a just and peaceful world.

The communal awakening, especially in third world regions, has brought the faith communities into direct confrontation with their national authorities. They no longer assume that the cure of souls will fulfill their obligation to God and the well-being of their peoples. They now recognize that political religions are often in direct conflict with their heritages of faith. This does not mean that religions of national identity are utterly discredited, although some theological movements such as Barthianism and neoorthodoxy have attempted to recover the confessional monopoly of religious life by discounting all other expressions of faith. The upshot of the struggle is that national or civil religions will be supported so long as they embody struggles for justice and peace. This is the prophetic stance that is now taking hold in the faith communities.

Many factors have contributed to this transformation in religious life. The two world wars brought an end to the optimistic mood of the West. More poignantly the Holocaust and the atomic bombing of Hiroshima and Nagasaki discredited claims about Western virtue. Meanwhile, whole regions of the world were slowly drawn into destitution and hunger, all in the name of development. As the faith communities began to share in this misery and struggle, they talked about solidarity with the poor and engaged in direct action with those who were trying to overcome their poverty and misery. This prophetic ministry also placed the confessional bodies in direct confrontations with their governments, often at great cost and sacrifice. A new religious politics was emerging and its outlines were far from clear.

The confessional bodies are not, in fact, the vanguard of these new movements for reform. They are participants in a struggle that reaches far beyond any traditional commitments. The faith communities are sharing in the emergence of new political religions, over against the traditional civil religions that undergird their national authorities. There are now two expressions of national religion. The civil religions of the national security states are symbolized largely in pledges of allegiance and other forms of loyalty oaths. The gist of these religious expressions is "My country, right or wrong!" The new political religions are movements of the poor for liberation from hunger, disease, and early death. The confessional bodies are actually divided in their loyalties to these two types of national religions. Some are deeply committed to the older nationalisms of the Western project. They support nuclear warfare in defense of their interests and live comfortably with military regimes that torture and kill their citizens. Others are beginning to share in the struggle for justice and peace, risking their own institutional resources by challenging the strategies of the national security states.

An awareness of the communal reality of human and divine life is a basic force in the new prophetic spirit. This awareness has come from the experience of solidarity in the struggle of the poor, so it reaches deeply into the spiritual life of these bodies. However, there is also consciousness of the dangers of plunging into another orgy of political religion, like National

Socialism in Germany and Fascism in Italy. A tension between loyalty to a divine mandate and sharing in the struggle for justice is evident in many of the writings of the liberation theologians. Leonardo and Clovodis Boff reflect this tension in their book *Salvation and Liberation*, in which they draw out the convergences and divergences of these two experiences of divine grace. In a somewhat similar vein, the theologians of the Philippines and Southeast Asia speak of a "theology of struggle," indicating their commitment to share in a long-term struggle for justice no matter what the immediate promise of deliverance. They are primarily concerned with solidarity in the struggle for justice.[1]

These religious transformations remain enigmatic unless they are set within the context of the new communalism that is taking hold throughout the world. Centuries of resignation to oppression and poverty are passing away with this transformation in political and religious vision. A sense of global solidarity and interdependence is inspiring civil and confessional movements with hope for a new world order. These are not the hopes of armchair academics or intellectuals who are ensconced in the institutes that shelter them. These are the thoughts and feelings that have come out of years of struggle and suffering. They lift up new themes in the West and throughout the world. Three of these themes are significant in identifying the quality of the new communalism that is appearing in our time.

Community with Nature

Community with nature is a guiding theme in the new theology. It challenges an earlier Christian preoccupation with a sinful and fallen world. Christian concern with sin was a departure from biblical affirmations of the goodness of creation. During the Hellenistic era, Christian salvation came to be expressed in terms of a "cleansing" from sin and a "spiritualizing" of human life in an idealistic sense. This orientation placed the human at the disposal of the church, which could offer a way through this vale of tears, with hope for release at the end of time. Natural impulses and feelings were shunned or carefully disciplined. Governance was to be left in the hands of those who had been destined for rule by an all-powerful deity, since the mass of people were incapable of caring for their own affairs.

The new ecology challenges this tradition at its very core, disclosing the importance of embodied life and our place within nature. We have interpreted this new impulse in terms of the artistic quality of the human being. People are seen as creative beings who can bring forth good works, share with nature in a cosmic creative process, and suffer with nature the pains of change and mortality. This means viewing humans as co-creators with God in a kind of cosmogenesis. The dignity of the human being, of every human being, is affirmed without depriving the natural world of its worth. Respect for all beings comes forth with creational responsibility. The novelty of this new religious consciousness is its awareness of power to shape natural as well as human destiny. We humans belong within the earth as nature belongs within us.

This creational understanding also yields new insight into the very being of the Divine Mystery. God, as the Christian West has usually named the Sacred Mystery, is no longer a remote, impassive, unchanging Being. If we share with the creator in the genesis of the cosmos, the world is open and God is freely limited by sharing our partnership and our freedom. God, too, dwells with a future that *is not*. Further, we are not separate from God. We are inwardly bonded with the Mystery as we are with all of life. This bonding does not take away from God's Being as Mystery, any more than our bonds with one another erase our own personal being. We are not defective creatures who are defined by our lack of the all-powerful goodness of the creator. We dwell within the spiritual creativity of the Mystery, even as the Spirit dwells within us. This spirituality of all being is not a retreat into idealism. It is an earthy, historical spirituality that informs our loving, working, and deciding. The Divine Mystery is closer to us than we are to our own being. Yet we are creatures and the Sacred Mystery is ever beyond, beckoning and luring us to fuller life and responsibility. In this consciousness, God is cosmic artistry unfolding a world. God is the metaphoric process of creation, disclosing a world and bringing a world to be out of the nonworld of possibilities, or, as the tradition has it, out of nothingness. This view contrasts radically with that of an all-powerful sovereign who manages the world like a cosmic programmer. A mature historical age has begun to throw off its dependence upon such a manipulator of human destiny. As the Dutch pastoral psychologist Heije Faber phrased it, we are now leaving the "Father House," the hostel where we were tucked in at night and kept safe.

The demise of the sovereign patriarch creates a troubling theological question in our communal age. How and in what ways does God enter into the painful struggles that plague all human life? There is no simple answer to such a question. However, there is a growing sense among religious people in this age that God's presence is empowering and sustaining in the midst of our joys and sorrows. This inspiriting presence is mediated by persons, communities, and such larger structures of care as economic and political institutions. Such strengthening presence is dramatically embodied in the hospice movement, a communal sharing in the difficult passage from life to death that enables the dying to share their stories and rework their pasts for this mysterious future. In these personal encounters, the power of the Divine Mystery pours creative energy into the daily round. Rather than displacing God from the ordinary business of life, the new sense of the Mystery brings an earthy nearness of spirituality that is close to the mystical tradition in the major faith communities of the world.

Community of Body and Mind

Community of body and mind is another theme in the communal age. This new unity of personhood is closely interwoven with a creational understanding of the human. However, this is a distinct strand in the new orientation. In a high-tech society, left-brain planning and analytic thought become the be-all and end-all of education and human development. We already noted this emphasis in the current theories of moral development. Imagination, moods, feelings, and sensibilities have been treated as weaknesses or defects. The successful bureaucrat is the one who can suppress all feeling, coping with every brutality that is imposed upon him or her. This is the true bureaucratic mind. To know this mind, one only has to see and hear the spokespersons of the United States departments of state and defense on television. They speak the impersonal language of the war system, referring to "subholocaust engagements" to describe the annihilation of less than tens of millions of people.[2]

The feminist movement has contributed richly to this disclosure of the wholeness of personal being. In their struggle for respect and a voice in the conduct of their affairs, women are creating a new understanding of the being of persons and communities. From the position of an oppressed community, women recognized that feelings were made their bailiwick by sexist organization, confining them to the private realm of family and neighborhood, defining them as unfit for business or public responsibility. In the eighteenth and nineteenth centuries intellectuals of the Enlightenment viewed black people as less than rational. They held the same prejudices toward women. Whatever did not fit the culture of white males was assumed to fall outside of the realm of rationality. This so-called rationality was, of course, profoundly shaped by feelings and moods, prejudices and interests, but that fact could be concealed so long as it could be assumed that this way of thinking was "scientific" thought, and, therefore, rational.

As the most immediate victims of this white male culture, women have opened whole new horizons of understanding of personal, moral, and political life through their insights into the interplay of mind and body, thought and sexuality, rational plans and desires. Western difficulties with sexuality, and it would not be difficult to document them, can certainly be traced to this spurious rationality and the suppression of feeling that has characterized our educational systems. We are sexual beings throughout our mental and physical lives, for we are loving beings who develop through interpersonal bonding. These are powerful forces in life which need to be disciplined but not repressed. Loving care is as fundamental to community building as right relations and wise planning. Only an appreciation of the wholeness of personhood can begin to break the iron grip of impersonal rationality on our schools and political economy.

The feminist movement is a countercultural revolution. It opens the way to intimacy and dialogue because it celebrates receptivity as well as activity, hearing as well as speaking, understanding as well as doing. Play, imagination, pleasure, feeling, and enjoyment now find an appropriate place in unfolding full rationality. After all, rational thought is the attunement of human process to the rhythms of natural and cosmic life. These rhythms are also the common infrastructure that creates a moral world which all peoples share, no matter how diverse the particular codings and symbolizations. The most rigorous sciences and the most exquisite artistic creations are human expressions of these rhythms, as John Dewey pointed out many years ago in his classic work *Art as Experience*. Moods and feelings often tell us more about what is going on than the ideas or facts that we accumulate. This is not to deny the importance of information. It is simply to recognize that our notion of fact is much too narrow. Facts depend upon interpretation of data, and that means that the whole of our language and experience enter into the formation of our factual world.

The new religious consciousness discerns receptivity and feeling in the Divine Mystery. There is strong biblical warrant for this insight, though it has been suppressed at times and almost totally erased in the West, except within the mystical tradition. Abraham Heschel drew attention to this "pathos" of God, as he called it, in his study *The Prophets*. This is to suggest that God is the Supreme Artist, receptive to all of being and creative in that very receptivity. This new/old image of the person as receptive as well as actively creative is captured in the view of the human as artistic being. Artistic sensibility not only shapes a work, it also sees, hears, feels, and understands in the course of creation. The artist is not some freak or special species, however gifted he or she may be. The artist is every person, whether that art is expressed in care of a youngster or fixing a meal or cutting a tool or composing a symphony. Matthew Fox brings out this truth of the human vividly in his fascinating book, *Original Blessing*. He cites a striking reference to this human way of being from Eric Gill, "Every artist may not be a special kind of person, but every person is a special kind of artist."[3]

Perhaps the greatest obstacle to our assuming our creative capacities as artists is the fear of taking responsibility for our lives and our world. Where such responsibility is assumed, we can see signs of the working of the Spirit, lifting the human to its full potential. When our creative drives are repressed, usually by the structures in which we live and work, we become depressed. There are fascinating stories of nineteenth-century English women who spent months under severe constraints while at home and then undertook adventures in distant lands that most men would never have risked. We were meant to be our own persons, but we need communal structures to support and encourage us in becoming who we really are. Co-creation is a work of freedom in community. It calls for receptivity as well as activity, sensible feelings as well as aggressive thought and action. Communal sensibility means hearing as well as speaking, following the fundamental rhythms of the cosmos. Violations of this basic, metaphoric rhythm occur constantly, to be sure, but when they do, and especially when they are incorporated into institutions, they disfigure and cripple life.

Communion in the Spirit

Communion in the Spirit is another element in the new religious reality. It is displacing the modern view of progress. This is in many ways the most radical repudiation of modernity in the new religious communalism. The past few centuries were marked by pride in scientific rationality and industrial productivity. With the emergence of Darwinian evolutionary theory, and possibly in part contributing to the readiness of Europe for the theory, trust in science and reason joined hands with confidence in social progress. Achievements in science, industry, and technique were celebrated as indicators of the inevitable progress of the human species, especially under the leadership of the West. A kind of social Darwinism captured the popular imagination. Confessional faith in the final coming of the Kingdom of God was transposed into public faith in human progress. This naive confidence in progress is gradually losing its grip on the religious consciousness.

To question inevitable progress is neither to despair of human possibilities nor to settle for private concerns. This questioning is rooted in a sense of the creational presence of the Mystery in every aspect and moment of life. This sense of communion in the Spirit creates a powerful impulse to reshape the public world. All of life now shares in communion through the Spirit. Improvement in personal and social life is recognized as a legitimate goal of religious and political life, yet there are no illusions about the destructive forces that constantly undermine such hopes. Building healthy communities and creating mutuality of life become priorities. This may mean, however, that religious leaders spend their lives and ministries in barrios and ghettos among impoverished and needy people, as is happening more and more in Latin America. Moreover, such religious leadership is no longer confined to agents of confessional bodies. Life is not defined in terms of gaining "power" and affluence. Life is first and last communion with another, with the larger community in its struggles for justice and peace, and with the Divine Mystery.

History takes on a very different character when communion in the Spirit becomes the hallmark of faith. Faith in progress, like the trickle-down theory of capitalistic economics, leaves the present lives of poor, hungry, and suffering people on the scrap heap of history. In conventional theories of progress, the lives of the poor are meaningful only as instruments for capital accumulation by the powerful. The illusion is that such sacrifices by the poor would ultimately bring the good life to future generations. Progress, like pie-in-the-sky Christianity, leaves life on earth pretty much to the affluent and powerful. The sufferings of life become a kind of pointless waiting for a glorious day which never materializes. History becomes, as Hegel observed, a butcher's block on which lives are slaughtered for the sake of a future civilization.

When communion in the Spirit becomes central to religious faith, we can understand how peoples in all times and cultures, however archaic their skills or advanced their technology, have the opportunity for spiritual empowerment. Life may have been more difficult in one era or region than in others, but loving, working, and deciding create communion with neighbors and nature at each point in the course of human history. Even suffering has its place in the communion of the Spirit. The suffering imposed by social forces of oppression is evil and destructive. It has to be resisted, yet even such suffering can be incorporated into the community of struggle, as is happening in liberation movements.

Concern for communion in the Spirit gives a special cast to the religious penetration of politics in this new era. The Eternal is experienced in and through whatever joys or sufferings may come in the struggle for justice and peace. The pain that informs all of life is integral to communion in the Spirit. Manipulative "power" politics is irrelevant to the political agenda of the new religious impulse. A manipulative gain in control does little to build a better community and often does more harm than good. This does not deny the place for challenging oppressive authority and possibly being driven to resistance, as has happened to the African National Congress under the duress of violence in South Africa. However, as Archbishop Tutu, Dom Helder Camara, and others have argued amid these struggles, the issue is how a community of responsible people can be built. In community building, as in most things, the ends always look strangely like the means that are used to achieve them. John Dewey stressed this point, for he believed firmly in the prime importance of communication and community as integral to any democracy. Violence is, at best, an evil that is forced on the community by the violence of oppressors. It can in no way become a means to the real building of community. Mahatma Gandhi understood this better than any revolutionary leader. When communion is primary, faith communities can contribute to the building of a healthy political life.

Sharing with nature, wholeness of body and mind, religious politics, and communion in the Spirit are interwoven strands of religion in a communal age. They reflect a new/old affirmation of creation. The common thread weaving these strands together is an earthy and spiritual building of community. If this religious impulse continues to gain momentum, it will certainly challenge political and economic oppression in our time. However, this description of the new religious mind leaves unanswered the more difficult question of how religious and political bodies differ. No matter how much they may share in the common task of community building, faith communities and political bodies are different expressions of human capacities and spirituality.

Prophetic Ministries in a Pluralistic World

The new ministries of confessional bodies are the real source of the new religious vision. Solidarity with the poor has begun to transform the minds and hearts of the faithful. Religious leaders have gradually been weaned from their age-old practice of telling and directing. They have been participants in a dialogue in which they are learning as much as or more than they are teaching. In this sense, the prophetic ministry has embodied the communion of the Spirit that is now the hallmark of the theologies of struggle. This is the reality of true dialogue. It is a way of being that embodies democratic communalism as well as celebrating it.

This experience of communal dialogue gives a clue to the task of confessional communities in the public realm. So long as they follow a dialogical course, they will not fall into the trap of promoting a political religion. They can thus become a reservoir of spiritual energy and insight in the struggle for justice and peace.

The confessional contribution to political life is grounded in a special receptivity. Religious life arises in divine disclosures that are inscribed in sacred texts. This is the source of the receptivity of faith communities. In our age, it is the revelation of the bondedness of all of life that has opened the way to a new communal life. Receptivity to that disclosure has moved the churches of Latin America into a new relationship with the poor, creating a dynamic of loving concern for all of life. Receptivity and solidarity with the poor generate the spirituality of these communities of faith. In this sense, receptivity is the expression of loving, the dynamic that sustains our solidarity with nature, one another, and the creative life of the Spirit.

By contrast, political life arises in the freedom to shape history through judgments and decisions. Politics is a work of active deliberating and deciding, however much its vitality is rooted in receptivity to its origins and hopes. In this sense the links between faith and politics are expressions of the relations between loving and deciding, between primary receptivity and primary activity. The interpenetration of faith and politics in our communal age can be constructive so long as it is guided by a dialogue between loving and deciding. It becomes totalitarian when this tension between receptivity and activity is violated. Faith communities embark upon political religion when they assume sovereignty. Political bodies become messianic agencies when they assume a sacred mantle. However, it would be historically erroneous to suggest that faith communities have always stood against political religion, while political communities have lost touch with the loving bonds that make politics a communal possibility. Political communities have often called confessional bodies away from their sectarian conflicts, reminding them of their true vocations. The interplay of loving and deciding runs through all personal and communal structures. We traced the inner dynamics of this interplay in the difficult decisions about abortion. We find a similar interplay in the primary tasks of faith communities and political bodies. Just as deciding brought many women in making their decisions to a new experience of loving concern, political bodies have often had to remind faith communities of their work of solidarity when they became preoccupied with the pursuit of power.

Faith and politics are inwardly bonded, as is evident in the spiritual origins of political communities and the concern for active service in all confessional bodies. Both communities share in the receptive and active dimensions of life. However, they have different charters. This difference in central principle means that their relations are always fraught with tension. The prophets constantly contended with the kings in Israel, calling them to their vocation as representatives of Yahweh's justice and peace. Prophetic challenge to political communities is confessional testimony to God's justice and peace. Faith communities are not political bodies, no matter how much they have acted like them at times. The political expression of the faith community is its prophetic word and deed. By the same token, the celebration of national days such as Thanksgiving and Memorial Day expresses the religious dynamic of political bodies. Prophetic sensitivity keeps the faith community in touch with its divine mandate. Religious celebration keeps the political body in touch with its origins. Neither community, however, has a monopoly on the grace that sustains all of life.

The founders of the Republic of the United States of America maintained the unity of faith and politics, yet preserved the difference between them through a series of decisions. These statements were metaphoric formulations. They were so basic to the future of the Republic that they became established symbols. The symbol, as we observed with such a symbol as God the Father, may suppress its metaphoric character. Then, it becomes an identity without a difference, and can become a dogma or a closed absolute. This has not been the case with the formulation of the relation of confessional faith and politics in the Republic. That has continued to be a tensive, creative relation throughout our history.

The Declaration of Independence was the first stage in the formulation. The unity of religion and politics was affirmed in the most general sense as follows:

> . . . We hold these truths to be self-evident, that all men are created equal, that they are endowed by their Creator with certain unalienable Rights, that among these are Life, Liberty, and the pursuit of Happiness.

The Constitutional Convention in 1787 decided to forego a religious test for public office, thus establishing a separation of confessional religion and politics. This separation or difference was confirmed in the First Amendment to the Constitution:

> Congress shall make no law respecting an establishment of religion, or prohibiting the exercise thereof; or abridging the freedom of speech, or of the press; or the right of the people peaceably to assemble, and to petition the Government for a redress of grievances.

In these propositions a distance was established between confessional faith and politics. At the same time, freedom of faith communities was guaranteed. The two communities would dwell, henceforth, in a tensive unity that proved enriching for both of them.

The new Republic achieved a metaphoric resolution of the relations between the confessional and political communities. The Republic acknowledged that human liberties and rights were anchored in a totality of life and creation. The Republic affirmed its separation, as political community, from the faith communities. This metaphoric tension has been preserved through a series of decisions in which the Supreme Court adjudicated the conflicting claims of confessional bodies and the defenders of separation. While presidents have asserted again and again the unity of religion and politics, invoking God in their inaugural addresses, the tensive interplay between the two communities has been maintained. This has been the charter of liberty for various confessional and nonconfessional groups. It has also made possible a pluralistic democracy.

Confessional and political bodies are expressions of two aspects of the artistic life, each stressing one side while sharing in the other. Artistic creation is a matter of receptive sensibility and creative making. A successful work combines these two aspects in a fine harmony, responding to the world and yet refashioning that world in such a way as to reveal previously hidden elements. Religion, like an artistic work, combines both of these dimensions, yet its virtue is the power of renewing a people's attunement to its world. Politics, the art of making and shaping, decays when it loses its artistic capacity to hear and understand, yet its virtue is the creative work of making a future possible. The art of community building requires both of these dimensions, religious and political. Under great stress, people lend greater weight to the receptive side of their heritage, turning toward traditionalism in religion and politics. This seems to be one of the dynamics of fundamentalism throughout the world. If carried too far, it can lead to political paralysis just when there is need for reshaping the future. In the euphoria of vital creativity, on the other hand, peoples turn toward the future without much regard for their heritage. This seems to have been one of the major forces at work in the modern era, a kind of intoxication with the achievements of science and the growing power of industry. This also can be damaging, for it can lead to an uprooting of people from the vital sources of their strength and a kind of mechanical repetition of actions that prove less and less fruitful. Perhaps a true harmony of receptivity and activity is never achieved except in the greatest works of art. Nevertheless, the overlap and difference of religion and politics seems to inhere in this tension between receptivity and activity, a tension that the Republic mandated in its charter of separation within unity.

There is a desperate search by peoples throughout the world for a hopeful future, often under conditions of extreme poverty and imminent death. This search has taken a religious as well as political form, bringing to the powerful nations an awareness that they share the world with many peoples and faiths. Whether they can learn to respect these other traditions remains to be seen. Unless they can appreciate these other cultures and traditions, it will be all but impossible to establish a peaceful world.

The spread of the global market has prepared the way for a new global community. The coalescence of religious and political communities in struggles for independence may be a harbinger of this new, global community. At this stage, the integrity of particular peoples and their religious heritages are being asserted. That very assertion may awaken the industrialized world to its responsibility to develop stable and equitable markets, appropriate technologies for various areas, and support for the third world in recovering control of its own lands, skills, and resources. These transformations will not come easily to the possessive societies of the Northern Hemisphere. However, a new religious vision in both the industrialized world and the third world may pave the way for a communal age and global citizenship. This could open a path to worldwide justice and peace, if the powerful states are able to shed their imperialistic pretensions and religious arrogance. This means a new dawning of receptive, loving concern, and a triumph of communalism over possessiveness. It would reflect a religious and political renaissance that could reopen the future. Such a new path to peace would be a promising fulfillment of the tensive bonds of loving and deciding in religious politics. It could create the conditions for a democratic communalism in economic and political life.

Notes

Chapter 1 / Movements of Communal Transformation

1. Sidney Mead, *The Lively Experiment: The Shaping of Christianity in America*, 1st edition (New York: Harper and Row, 1963).

2. Robert N. Bellah et al., *Habits of the Heart* (Berkeley: University of California Press, 1985), p. 142.

3. Zsuza Hegedus, "The Challenge of the Peace Movement: Civilian Security and Civilian Emancipation," *Alternatives* 12, no. 2 (1987): 197-216.

Chapter 2 / The Web of Life

1. J. Larry Brown, "Hunger in the U.S.," *Scientific American* 256, no. 2 (February 1987): 37–41.

2. Beverly Harrison, *Our Right to Choose: Toward an Ethic of Abortion* (Boston: Beacon Press, 1983), p. 214.

3. Ibid., pp. 220f.

4. Carol Gilligan, "Do the Social Sciences Have an Adequate Theory of Moral Development," in *Social Science as Moral Inquiry*, ed. Norma Haan, Robert N. Bellah, Paul Rabinow, and William M. Sullivan (New York: Columbia University Press, 1983), pp. 33–51; see also Carol Gilligan, *In A Different Voice* (Cambridge: Harvard University, 1982).

5. This more foundational view of justice has been explored by Charles Amjad-Ali of the Christian Study Centre in Pakistan; see also Roger Hutchinson, "Mutuality: Procedural Norm and Foundational Symbol," in *Liberation and Ethics*, ed. Charles Amjad-Ali and Alvin Pitcher (Chicago: Center for the Scientific Study of Religion, 1985), and Beverly Harrison, "The Power of Anger in the Work of Love," in *Making the Connections*, ed. Carol S. Robb (Boston: Beacon Press, 1985), pp. 3–21.

6. Daniel and Sidney Callahan, "Abortion: Understanding Our Differences," *Update* 2, no. 2 (March 1986): 3–6.

Chapter 3 / The Moral Web

1. Karsten Harries, "Metaphor and Transcendence," in *On Metaphor*, ed. Sheldon Sacks (Chicago: University of Chicago Press, 1979), pp. 71–88.

Chapter 4 / The Organization of Work

1. Jonathan Kozol, "The Homeless and Their Children," *The New Yorker*, 1 February 1988, pp. 36–67.
2. Alasdair MacIntyre, *After Virtue* (Notre Dame: University of Notre Dame Press, 1984), pp. 187–96.
3. Ibid., p. 196.
4. Benjamin Barber, "What Do 47-Year Olds Know," *The New York Times*, 26 December 1987, Op ed page.
5. National Conference of Catholic Bishops, *Economic Justice for All: A Pastoral Letter on Catholic Social Teaching and The U.S. Economy* (Washington, D.C.: United States Catholic Conference, 1986), p. v.
6. Urban Coalition of the Episcopal Church, U.S.A., "Economic Justice and the Christian Conscience," 10 October 1987, pp. 18f.
7. John C. Raines and Donna C. Day-Lower, *Modern Work and Human Meaning* (Philadelphia: Westminster Press, 1986), pp. 114–16.

Chapter 5 / A Politics of Community Building

1. J. Larry Brown, "Hunger in the U.S.," *Scientific American* 256, no. 2 (February 1987): 37–41.
2. Susan George, *How the Other Half Dies: The Real Reasons for World Hunger* (Totowa, N.J.: Rowman and Allanheld, 1977), p. 161.
3. Gar Alperovitz and Jeff Faux, *Rebuilding America* (New York: Pantheon Books, 1984), p. 192.
4. Center for Defense Information, Washington, D.C., *The Defense Monitor* 16, no. 7 (1987): 1–3.
5. Barry Bluestone, "Deindustrialization and the Abandonment of Community," in *Community and Capital in Conflict: Plant Closings and Job Loss*, ed. John C. Raines, Leonora E. Berson, and David McI. Gracie (Philadelphia: Temple University Press, 1982), pp. 41–44.
6. Nicholas Georgescu-Roegen, "The Entrophy Law and the Economic Problem," in *Toward a Steady-State Economy*, ed. Herman E. Daly (San Francisco: W. H. Freeman, 1973), p. 47.
7. "Arms Spending," *Sojourners*, 18 April 1988, p. 15.

Chapter 6 / Religious Transformations

1. Lester E. J. Ruiz, "Theology, Politics and the Discourse of Transformation," *Alternatives* 13, no. 2 (1988): 155–76.

2. Carol Cohn, "Sex and Death in the Rational World of Defense Intellectuals," *Signs* 12, no. 4 (1987): 703–7.

3. Matthew Fox, *Original Blessing* (Santa Fe., N.M.: Bear and Co., 1983), p. 188.